1100, 1300 HANDYBOOK

Owner's Handbook for
Austin 1100, 1300 Mk 1, 2, 3 from 1963
Austin America, 1300 GT from 1969
Austin 1100, 1300 Countryman from 1966
Morris 1100, 1300, GT Mk 1, 2 1962-71
Morris 1100, 1300 Traveller 1966-73
MG 1100, 1300 Mk 1, 2 1962-71
Riley Kestrel 1100, 1300 Mk 1, 2 1965-69
Vanden Plas Princess 1100, 1300 from 1963
Wolseley 1100, 1300 Mk 1, 2 1965-73

by

Kenneth Ball

Associate Member, Guild of Motoring Writers

and the

Autopress team of Technical Writers

AUTOPRESS LTD   GOLDEN LANE   BRIGHTON   BN1 2QJ   ENGLAND

INTRODUCTION

This do-it-yourself Owner's Handbook has been specially written for the owner with little or no previous experience, who wishes to carry out his own day-to-day maintenance and servicing. Considerable savings on garage charges can be made and one can drive in safety and confidence knowing the work has been done properly and that the car is in first-class condition.

Simple but comprehensive step-by-step instructions and illustrations are given on all servicing operations, tuning and adjustment.

Throughout the Handbook hints and tips are included and there is an easy to follow, solve-it-yourself chapter which will be found invaluable.

Whilst every care has been taken to ensure correctness of information it is obviously not possible to guarantee complete freedom from errors or to accept liability arising from such errors or omissions.

Instructions may refer to the righthand or lefthand sides of the vehicle or the components. These are the same as the righthand or lefthand of an observer standing behind the car and looking forward.

ISBN 0 85147 814 X

First Edition   1973
Second Edition, fully revised   1974

© Autobooks Ltd 1974

Printed and bound in Brighton England for Autobooks Ltd by G Beard & Son Ltd

B

CONTENTS

GETTING ACQUAINTED

:1 Introduction

Many people are surprised to learn that the first 100 was produced more than a decade ago. This was he Morris 1100 introduced in August 1962, after he unrivalled success of the Mini. When one coniders that there have been no major changes in esign since then, the latest Mk 3 version being ery much the same as the original Mk 1, it proves he soundness and popularity of the design. There ave been mechanical improvements, of course, nd different models from the sister 'stables' of ustin, MG, Wolseley and Riley, including the uxurious prestige model, the Vanden Plas Princess.

The 1100 was designed by Alex Issigonis, then MC's chief designer, using the same ideas that had roved so successful in the Mini. Like its smaller ister the 1100 has an engine that is located in an ast-west position, in other words the engine is nounted across the car instead of longitudinally as in n orthodox car. The engine and transmission are nounted as one unit at the front of the car and the rive is transmitted to the front wheels.

The simple fact of placing the engine across the ar allows almost 80 per cent of the car's length to e used for passengers and luggage. In this way the ear passengers have much more leg room. Unlike onventional cars with the drive to the rear wheels, here is only a low 'hump' in the middle of the floor t the back.

The Hydrolastic system is a unique concept in suspension design, the result of intensive research by Alex Moulton, who is also famous for the small-wheeled bicycle. It consists of four rubber 'springs' which are mounted at each corner of the car, the front and rear units on either side being connected by a liquid-filled pipe.

Each side works independently of the other. To understand how the hydrolastic system works, imagine the front wheel riding over a bump (see **FIG 1:4**). The upward movement of the wheel deflects the rubber 'spring' and forces liquid through the interconnecting pipe to the rear unit on the same side. The effect of this is to raise the rear of the car by the same amount as the front and thus maintain the car on an even keel. When the rear wheel meets the same bump the whole process is reversed. This reduces the 'pitching' at the front and rear of the vehicle when it is being driven on bumpy roads.

The engine is a four-cylinder unit, with either one or two carburetters according to model. The two-carburetter version gives extra power and is fitted to the MG, Riley, Wolseley and Princess cars. This engine has been well proven for reliability and performance, having first been used in the Morris Minor 1000. The power was increased by the introduction in October 1967 of the 1300 which was fitted with a 1275 cc engine with a single carburetter.

FIG 1:1 Morris 1100 Mk 1 four-door saloon, 1962–67

The gearbox has an improved synchromesh system on all forward speeds, with the exception of first gear on some of the earlier models. Gearchanging is by a central, floor-mounted gearlever. An alternative method of gear shifting was available as an optional extra with the advent of an automatic transmission system in October 1965.

To complete the range, Austin and Morris introduced estate car models, the Countryman and the Traveller. They have the roof extended rearwards to a one-piece opening tailgate. The rear seats can be folded down to give a large load-carrying platform.

The following section is a summary of all the models.

1:2 Summary of models

It is often very useful to be able to identify a particular model, especially when buying a secondhand car. For that reason we are giving major changes in specification in the following summary. Further information and new and secondhand prices will be found in the monthly 'MOTORISTS GUIDE'.

FIG 1:2 Vanden Plas Princess 1100 Mk 1 four-door saloon, 1963–67

August 1962:

Morris 1100 Mk 1 (2 or 4 doors) 1098 cc engine and a fourspeed gearbox having synchromesh on 2nd, 3rd and 4th gears. Front wheel disc brakes.

October 1962:

MG 1100 Mk 1 (2 or 4 doors). Similar to the Morris 1100 Mk 1 but with twin carburetters, different front styling and some interior refinement.

September 1963:

Austin 1100 Mk 1 (2 or 4 doors). Similar to the Morris 1100 Mk 1, but with a different grille and facia.

October 1963:

Vanden Plas Princess Mk 1 introduced. Luxuriously appointed with walnut facia, extra gauges and much extra equipment. Mechanically identical to the MG.

September 1965:

Riley Kestrel 1100 Mk 1 and the Wolseley 1100 Mk 1 introduced. Identified by traditional grilles, special trim and facia panels. Both had 1098 cc engines with twin carburetters.

October 1965:

BMC's automatic transmission available as an optional extra on the Austin and Morris 1100 Mk 1.

March 1966:

The Austin Countryman 1100 and the Morris Traveller 1100 made their debut.

FIG 1:3 Austin 1100 Mk 2 two-door saloon, from 1967

May 1966:

Optional reclining front seats available on all models.

June 1967:

The 1275 cc engine offered as an optional extra on MG, Riley, Vanden Plas and Wolseley 1100 models until October of that year.

October 1967:

The Mk 2 1100 introduced for all models. The 1300 Mk 1 also introduced with the 1275 cc engine. Face lifting included restyled grilles, modified tail fins and rear lights, redesigned instruments, slotted wheels, repeater flashers on the sides of the wings and a combination switch mounted on the steering column.

The 1300 had a slightly different grille, a single-carburetter engine and an all-synchromesh gearbox. Automatic transmission an optional extra on MG, Riley, Vanden Plas and Wolseley.

January 1968:

The Riley 1100 Mk 2 was discontinued.

February 1968:

The Wolseley 1100 Mk 2 was discontinued.

March 1968:

Austin and Morris 1100 Mk 2 de-luxe 2-door and Super de-luxe 2- and 4-door, the 1300 de-luxe 2- and 4-door, the MG 1100, the MG 1300 Mk 1 4-door, and the Vanden Plas 1100 Mk 2 models were discontinued.

Early 1968:

1300 twin-carburetter engine on MG, Riley, Vanden Plas and Wolseley with manual transmission.

April 1968:

MG 1300 Mk 1 2-door models available until October 1968.

October 1968:

MG, Riley and Wolseley 1300 Mk 2 models with 1275 cc engine and twin carburetters. New facia on MG.

July 1969:

Riley Mk 2 1300 discontinued.

October 1969:

Austin and Morris 1300 GT introduced.

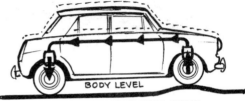

FIG 1:4 How the Hydrolastic suspension system works. Arrows on interconnecting pipe indicate direction of fluid transfer between suspension units

FIG 1:5 Austin 1300 two-door saloon, from 1967

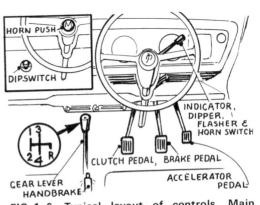

FIG 1:6 Typical layout of controls. Main illustration is of later Vanden Plas Princess. Inset shows variations of horn push and dip-switch on early Morris 1100

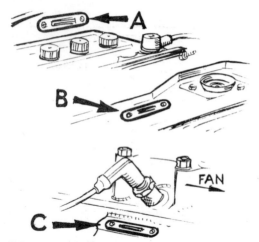

FIG 1:7 Identification plates. Commission number (A), car number (B) and engine number (C)

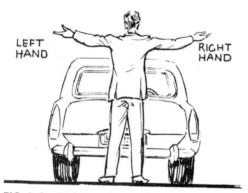

FIG 1:8 Righthand and lefthand locations of parts of the car are as viewed from behind, and looking forward

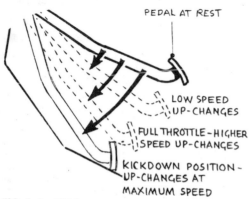

FIG 1:9 With automatic transmission, the position of the accelerator pedal affects gear-changing. For maximum acceleration the 'kick-down' position is used

1:3 Identification

Every car carries identification plates for the commission number, car or chassis number and the engine number. **Copy the numbers on a plain postcard, together with the key numbers and store the card safely in the house.** Key numbers are most important as the locks are not marked in order to reduce the possibility of theft.

The commission number is fixed to the righthand wing valance, just above the battery (see **FIG 1:7, A**).

The car number is located on the righthand side of the bonnet lock platform (see **FIG 1:7, B**).

The engine number is secured to the cylinder block under the sparking plug nearest to the fan (see **FIG 1:7, C**).

Throughout this manual there will be frequent references to the righthand or lefthand sides of the car. **There should be no difficulty in finding the locations if it is remembered that they are as viewed from behind the car, looking forward** (see **FIG 1:8**).

1:4 Gearlevers and gear selection

Manual gearlever (see FIG 1:6):

For manual operation an orthodox clutch must be used for getting away and for shifting from one gear to another. The lever positions are shown in the illustration and are also printed on the gearlever knob. Reverse cannot be engaged until resistance to sideways movement is overcome by pressing the lever fully to the right.

Automatic transmission lever:

The automatic transmission selector lever has a reverse stop. There is an early type in which the lever is lifted over a quadrant stop to engage reverse. On later cars the collar on the lever must be lifted before the lever can be moved into the reverse position.

The large number of positions marked on the selector quadrant may be puzzling to the owner who expects automatic transmission to take over all the gear-shifting. This, of course, it will do if the lever is left in the 'D' position. The other positions are provided to give manual control.

Starting (with automatic transmission):

Always apply the handbrake or footbrake before starting the engine. **The engine cannot be started unless the lever is in the 'N' position.** Having started a cold engine, let it warm up for half a minute, pushing the choke knob inwards from the rich mixture position as soon as possible, but keeping engine speed high to prevent stalling.

Moving off:

Never select a gear unless the engine is idling, or there may be a 'thump' from the transmission. For automatic drive select D. Move to 1 or 2 for manual gear selection. In D, all changes up or down will be automatic according to driving conditions and accelerator position. As automatic changing may not be ideal under all conditions, manual selection is provided so that the driver can change gear when circumstances demand it.

In any selected position except N, which is neutral, the car will be inclined to creep slightly when the brake is released with the engine running. This feature will be found very useful when manoeuvring the car in confined spaces or in slow-moving traffic. Depressing the accelerator pedal will make the car move off smoothly. If, during the running period before the engine has reached normal temperature it is necessary to use the footbrake, keep the right foot on the accelerator pedal so that some extra throttle can be applied to avoid stalling the engine. If the weather is very cold, drive a few hundred yards in a low gear such as 2 to get the engine and transmission warmed up quickly.

Normal driving:

If D has been selected so that all gearchanges are automatic, moderate pressure on the accelerator pedal will give upward changes at low speeds. Rapid pressure on the pedal up to full throttle position causes upward changes to be made at higher speeds. The pedal may be pressed still farther into the 'kick-down' position and this will produce upward changes at maximum road speeds to give the fastest acceleration (see **FIG 1:9**). However, when cruising in D and wanting increased acceleration, for example to pass another car, the pedal may be pressed through the 'kick-down' position to secure a downward change. Note that this downward change will not happen above certain speeds in order to protect the transmission. Third cannot be downshifted above 43 mile/hr, second above 34 mile/hr and first above 22 mile/hr. Manual selection must be used to get higher speeds in these three gears.

Manual selection:

When moving the lever freely from gear to gear remember that there is a limit to the speeds at which downshifting can be attempted. **Do not change down to third gear at a speed above 50 mile/hr, nor down to second gear above 40 mile/hr.**

Selecting neutral (N):

Do not select N when the car is moving, or there may be snatch if a forward gear is then engaged before the car has come to rest.

Descending steep hills:

Do not select bottom gear (1) for braking on steep hills. Second gear (2) is the lowest gear you can use (see **Section 1:12** for advice on towing).

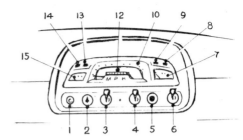

FIG 1:10 Instrument panel for early Morris 1100. To identify parts see Key below

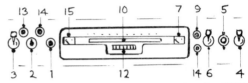

FIG 1:11 Instrument panel for Austin 1100 Mk 1. See Key below

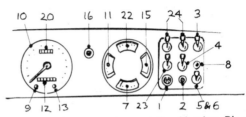

FIG 1:12 Instrument panel for Vanden Plas 1100 Mks 1 and 2 and 1300. See key below. Ignition and starter switch may be on steering column (later)

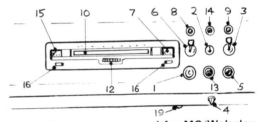

FIG 1:13 Instrument panel for MG/Wolseley 1100 Mks 1 and 2, 1300 Mk 1 and Wolseley 1300 Mk 2. Switches 6 and 3 may be 'flick' or 'rocker'

Key to FIGS 1:10 to 1:16 1 Choke 2 Ignition and starter 3 Lights 4 Panel lights 5 Windscreen washer 6 Wipers 7 Fuel gauge 8 Oil filter warning (amber) 9 Headlamp main beam warning (blue) 10 Speedometer 11 Oil pressure gauge 12 Mileage indicator 13 Ignition warning (red) 14 Oil pressure warning (amber) 15 Water temperature gauge 16 Direction indicator warning (green) 17 Tachometer 18 Spare warning light (white) 19 Bonnet release 20 Trip mileage 21 Trip reset 22 Ammeter 23 Heated rear window switch 24 Fog light switch 25 Warning light for heated rear window (green)

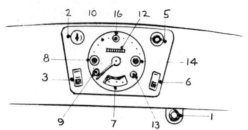

FIG 1:14 Instrument panel for Austin/Morris 1100 and 1300 Mk 2 and 1300 de-luxe. See Key on preceding page

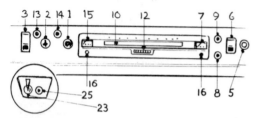

FIG 1:15 Instrument panel for Austin/Morris 1100/1300 Mk 2 and 1300 Super de-luxe. Key is on preceding page

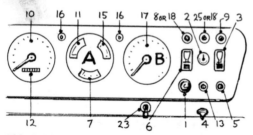

FIG 1:16 Instrument panel for Riley 1100 Mks 1 and 2 and 1300 Mk 1. Also for MG/Riley 1300 Mk 2 (on later cars A and B may be interchanged) Key is on preceding page. Switches 6 and 3 'flick' or 'rocker'

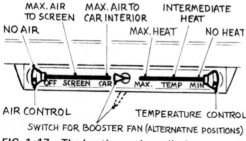

FIG 1:17 The heating and ventilating controls

Stopping:

Release the accelerator pedal and apply the brakes. It does not matter what position the lever is in.

Parking:

Stop the car, select N (neutral) and switch off the ignition. **Always apply the handbrake when the car is parked.**

1:5 Instrument panels

FIGS 1:10 to **1:16** show the different designs of instrument panels. The illustrations give the locations of the various warning lights, any changes being due to variations between the models. Some models have gauges instead of warning lights.

The ignition warning light:

Switch on the ignition and the red light will glow. It will continue to glow or flicker at very low engine speeds. If the car is fitted with an alternator the light will go out the moment the engine starts.

The light indicates that electrical current is being generated. If it fails to go out as the engine is speeded up, it is a sign of trouble. If it appears while motoring it is usually due to a broken belt.

Oil pressure warning light:

This is amber. It should go out in a second or two after starting the engine. If it does not, or glows suddenly while motoring, stop at once and check the oil level on the dipstick. If it does not go out with the engine running, switch off at once and investigate the trouble.

Oil filter warning light:

This is item 8 in the illustrations. If it glows above fast-idling engine speed, the filter is clogged or the oil needs changing (see **Chapter 5**).

Headlamp dipping, indicator and heated rear window warning lights:

The blue or green warning lights will glow when the switches are operated.

1:6 Hot or cold air ventilation

The controls are below the facia (see **FIG 1:17**). The lefthand lever controls air to the interior or the windscreen. CAR will give you maximum air to your feet and SCREEN gives air at windscreen level. Mid-positions will give shared delivery. Use SCREEN position for defrosting.

The righthand lever regulates air temperature. MAX position gives air that is heated. At MIN the air is cold. Select mid-positions for varying temperatures. Use MAX for defrosting.

Forward car movement will provide moderate hot or cold air as selected. To boost the air supply, switch on the fan by means of the central lever. With the lever to the right there is no fan output. With the lever central there is half-boost, and full-boost with the lever to the left. These positions are reversed on some models.

As there is no heated air until the engine has warmed up, leave the lefthand control at OFF for a mile or two.

Switch off the fan in traffic to avoid filling the car with unpleasant fumes.

Rear window demister:

If your car has a heated rear window, take care of the inner surface. Scratching or abrasion may damage the element.

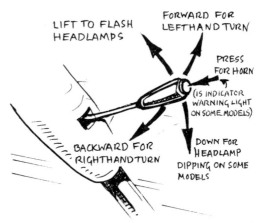

FIG 1:18 The steering column control switch. Note variations on extreme right

1:7 Steering column controls

There are many variations, the control lever shown in **FIG 1:18** being fitted to later models. Early Mk 1 cars may have green direction indicator warning lights on the facia or on the end of the indicator stalk. The horn may be operated by a push button in the centre of the steering wheel or by pressing the knob of the stalk inwards.

If the headlamp beams are not dipped by moving the stalk then the dipswitch is on the toe-board as shown by the inset in **FIG 1:6**. On full-beam a blue warning light glows on the facia.

1:8 Starting up

Before starting the engine put the gearlever in neutral and apply the handbrake. Select N if automatic transmission is fitted. Pull out the choke control if engine is cold.

Turn ignition key to first position. The red and amber warning lights will glow. If the ignition switch is on the column (see **FIG 1:19**) turn it to position 11. Further movement of the key will operate the starter. Release key when engine fires. Oil gauge should now register pressure or amber warning light should go out. **Do not operate the starter while the engine is running.**

After the engine has started, do not continue to run it with the choke knob pulled right out. Push the knob in slowly and the engine should keep running smoothly. If the weather is very cold the engine may have a tendency to die out, in which case it is permissible to pull out the choke knob a short way to keep it running.

To achieve the ideal of a fast warm-up it is necessary to keep the engine running at what is called a fast-idle, with no choke at all. This, you will find, is possible when the choke knob is almost fully pushed in. Actually the last $\frac{1}{4}$ to $\frac{1}{2}$ inch of movement will keep the engine running at a fast-idle without

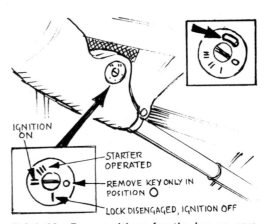

FIG 1:19 Four positions for the key on cars fitted with a steering column lock

FIG 1:20 Always check that the gearlever is in the neutral position before starting the engine

the choke operating (see **Chapter 4**). **Never let the engine idle slowly from cold as it will lead to rapid wear.** In fact, if it is not possible to let it warm-up at a fast-idle it is quite a good plan to use the car on the road at once.

If the engine will not start after several attempts it is wise to leave it for a short time and make a quick investigation of the possible causes (see the beginning of **Chapter 7**). Over-choking is a common cause of difficulty in starting and it is possible to overcome this problem by the method suggested. **Never, at any time, try to start a hot engine with the choke knob pulled out.** If a hot engine needs choke to start it there is something sadly wrong with its state of tune.

Continued use of the starter will eventually drain the battery, after which there will be no hope of starting without assistance. If the starter motor begins to labour, losing its initial briskness, stop and check for possible causes before the battery is flat.

As soon as the engine starts, check the oil pressure indicator and the ignition warning light. If either or both lights continue to glow at a fast-idle, stop the engine at once and find out the reason (see **Chapter 7**). Lack of oil pressure may be due to low oil level, and a broken belt may be the answer to the ignition light staying on.

If a temperature gauge is fitted, check that the needle rises gradually from the COLD position after the car has begun to warm up. It should move towards the HOT position and remain steady. If it continues to rise rapidly, check the water level in the radiator (see **Chapter 3**). Do not continue to run the engine until checking has pin-pointed the trouble. The gauge needle should drop back to the COLD position when the engine cools down.

The oil filter warning light on some models is intended as a guide to the need for oil and filter changing. If the light continues to glow when the engine is running it shows that the engine oil and the filter element should be changed (see **Chapter 5**). Do this within the next 300 miles.

1:9 Filling up

There should be no trouble with blow-back from the petrol tank filler when filling up. If there is, refer to **Chapter 7**. **Do not continue filling with petrol so that the fuel can be seen in the filler neck.** Parking the car at an angle may cause an overflow, or if it is left in the hot sun, expansion may have the same effect.

1:10 Running-in

You have bought a new car and you want to give it the best start in life. This is ensured in the early stages of its use on the roads. The treatment given to

a new car has an important bearing on its durabili and subsequent smooth running and it is strong recommended that you follow the maker's instruc tions on running-in speeds. These are:

For the first 500 miles keep the maximum spee below 45 mile/hr and never let the engine labou particularly when the car is heavily laden and yo are trying to climb a steep hill in a high gear. Drop t a lower gear to keep the engine running fairly fas under a light load. Do not operate at full pressure o the accelerator pedal for the first 500 miles. Th applies in any gear.

1:11 Fitting a roof rack

Do not carry more than 100 lb weight on a roo rack. It is preferable that such a load is well sprea out and does not consist of a small and very heav article.

1:12 Towing

The permissible weight that may be towed i 15 cwt for Saloon, Countryman and Traveller car with the exception of the Vanden Plas Princess wher the limit is 12 cwt. The downward load on the towin ball should be between 75 and 100 lb.

1:13 Buying a secondhand car

If the car is more than three or four years ol take expert advice. Normally there should be no ris if you buy from a reputable dealer, particularly on with a British Leyland franchise.

Buying privately needs more care, because even a expert may not spot a serious defect unless the ca is stripped right down. However, a knowledgeabl friend or garage mechanic should be able to find th obvious faults.

Be particularly wary of a car that shows signs o excessive wear of the carpets and general trim an is also going rusty along the sills under the door at the lower edges of the wings and just behind th headlamp rims. The most satisfactory way of buyin a secondhand car is to have it vetted by one of th AA or RAC engineers. The fee will be well worth it.

1:14 Performance tests

You may become uncomfortably aware that you car is down on performance compared with simila cars, or that the petrol consumption is excessiv In this case try to get a friend or a helpful garag mechanic to give you a second opinion. Readin **Chapter 7** may also give you some good ideas o improving both conditions.

If you would like to compare other performanc figures with your own, buy the test reports produce by the MOTOR and the AUTOCAR. Prices of th reports and addresses will be found in current issue

DOING IT YOURSELF

2:1 Making a start   2:2 Working safely   2:3 The tool kit   2:4 The stores   2:5 Testing after repairs

2:1 Making a start

A few decent tools and a modicum of skill will enable you to combat wear and tear by making simple repairs and adjustments. In this way you will benefit from improved performance, reduced running costs and longer life for your car.

This chapter tells you how to equip your workshop and how to take those sensible precautions that are needed to avoid certain hazards.

2:2 Working safely

Many precautions that will help you to work safely will be mentioned throughout this manual, but this section will cover the main points.

Fire:

We need hardly stress the danger of smoking or using a naked flame near petrol. If you are unfortunate enough to start a petrol fire, do not try to extinguish it with water. Use an extinguisher, or sand, or even earth. Electrical shorts are a common cause of fires, so always disconnect the battery before working on the system, particularly when wiring is to be detached.

Starting-up:

Always check the gearlever before operating the starter. This applies particularly if it is necessary to use the starter button under the bonnet. If the gearlever is not in neutral and the engine starts you may have the problem of a runaway car.

The danger from exhaust fumes:

This is the most insidious danger of them all. **Never run a car engine in a closed garage.** The carbon monixide in the exhaust gases may cause unconsciousness without warning, and if help is not immediately available the result could almost certainly be fatal. If the engine must be run, open the garage doors and push the rear end outside. **FIG 2:1** will emphasise this warning.

Keeping clear of moving parts:

When the engine is running it is dangerous to get too near the fan, the belt and the pulleys. Keep the hands clear of moving parts and take care that loose clothing such as a tie cannot be caught up.

Working with mains electricity:

Appliances that work from the mains supply must be properly earthed (see **FIG 2:2**). Garage floors are often damp and will provide a ready earth for a faulty appliance. When the floor is wet, stand on wood or wear thick rubber-soled shoes. Preferably use an inspection lamp that can be run off the car battery.

Jacking-up the car:

There are two types of jack, the column jack shown in **FIG 2:3** that is used on the 1100 and early 1300 models and the scissor jack shown in **FIG 2:4** that is used on the later 1300.

FIG 2:1 Never run the engine in a closed garage. Exhaust gases are highly toxic and may cause death

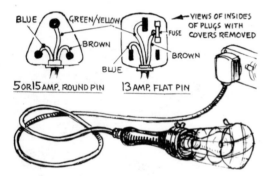

FIG 2:2 Appliances connected to the mains must be properly earthed. Insets of plugs show correct wiring colours

FIG 2:3 The original type of jack has a lifting arm that is inserted into a socket under the door sill

Before attempting to jack-up the car, satisfy yourself that it is standing on firm and level ground. Make sure the handbrake is fully applied and use bricks or wooden blocks to chock the wheels that are not being raised, unless the operation is no more than a simple wheel change. Slacken the wheel nuts half a turn before lifting the wheel clear of the ground. Fully tighten them when the car is off the jack. This will avoid excessive rocking when the car is raised. Make sure the jack arm is fully inserted in the socket.

The scissor jack can be located anywhere along the sill, but make sure the slot in the jack-pad fits the flange of the sill as shown in the illustration. If extensive work is to be carried out under the car, provide additional supports such as broad wooden blocks. **Do not use ordinary house bricks.** Place the support close to the jack. If blocks are used, build them up securely and as close to the sill as possible, so that in the event of the jack collapsing the car will only drop a fraction.

The sills of the car are prone to corrosion and rust. A badly corroded sill may collapse under the strain when the car is jacked-up. If you own an early model and have any doubts about its condition it is best to take no chance of being stranded with a flat tyre and no means of changing the wheel. In this case the way out of the difficulty is to invest in a screw-type or hydraulic jack. The only problem with these jacks is that they must be applied in a manner that will not damage the part they lift against. The answer to this problem is to approach your garage and get them to suggest suitable places where the jack may be used. In any case it is advisable to carry a short piece of thick wide plank to interpose between the jack head and the part of the car.

Jacking up a car on soft ground may present some difficulty due to the jack sinking in. Here again a short piece of thick wood will help to spread the load.

2:3 The tool kit

If you are prepared to tackle the tasks of tuning and adjusting the equipment on your car, a good tool kit is essential. Do not be tempted to use old spanners that do not fit, and do not buy cheap tools that are not properly hardened and will bend or wear out after a short time. Nothing is more exasperating than trying to work with inferior tools especially when a spanner slips and your knuckles are skinned!

Spanners:

The nuts and bolts on 1100 and 1300 models require AF spanners. The AF stands for 'American Fine' a widely used system of nut, bolt and thread sizes. The quoted dimension is the width between opposite flats of a nut or bolt. This will also be the width between the jaws of a spanner that fits, and the size is stamped on an adjacent part of the shank.

FIG 2:5 shows the various types of spanner, the simplest being the open-ended one. This will do useful work and is sometimes the only spanner that can be used in awkward places. A set should start at $\frac{3}{16}$ inch and go up in $\frac{1}{16}$ inch steps to $\frac{7}{8}$ inch. The spanners will be double-ended and the sizes will be duplicated except for the smallest and largest jaws of a set. The professional types of spanners are the ring and socket sets. These are powerful and safe to use because they do not slip readily. A comprehensive set of socket spanners and wrenches will be expensive, but ring spanners will be found adequate for most amateur jobs on the car. The simple box spanner is a cheap substitute for the socket spanner and will do useful work if it is not over-strained. Most sparking plug spanners are of this type. It is recommended that you try to get a plug spanner that has a rubber insert inside the tubular part. This will protect the ceramic insulator of the plug which is very easily broken if the spanner is allowed to tilt.

Screwdrivers:

The original type of slotted screw head needs a flat-bladed screwdriver of the type shown on the left. Due to the wide range of screw sizes it will be advisable to acquire widths from $\frac{1}{8}$ inch for electrical work and then by $\frac{1}{16}$ inch steps up to a width of $\frac{5}{16}$ inch. There are two types of crosshead screws and the heads are shown in the illustration. Check on the type fitted to your car and buy the correct type of screwdriver to fit. The most useful sizes will be $\frac{3}{16}$, $\frac{1}{4}$ and $\frac{5}{16}$ inch in diameter.

Additional equipment:

This is shown in **FIG 2:6**.

Pliers:

These may be bought in a variety of shapes and sizes but the two shown will probably cover all your needs.

Feeler gauges:

These are essential for measurements such as valve clearance and the gap between contact breaker points. The thin steel blades are marked in thousandths of an inch in a range that usually runs from 2 to 20 or 25.

Lubricating devices:

Buy a small tin of general-purpose thin oil such as 'Three-in-one'. The pump-type oil can is used with engine oil and can be controlled to give the quantity required. The simple push-type grease gun will do most jobs quite satisfactorily, but if you want extra power with modest effort buy one of the lever-operated type.

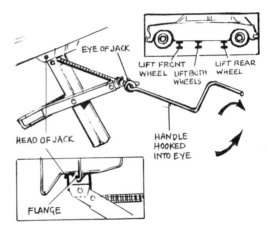

FIG 2:4 Later cars may have the scissors-type jack. Use in positions indicated (top right) to lift as required. Head of jack must fit over body flange (bottom left)

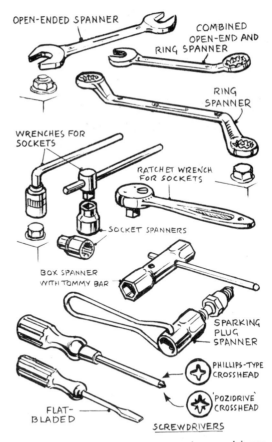

FIG 2:5 Types of spanners and screwdrivers for your basic tool kit. Check the screws on your car before buying the crosshead screwdriver

FIG 2:6 A further selection of useful items that will help to complete the basic tool kit

FIG 2:7 It is cheaper to buy oil in bulk. Do not store brake fluid in an open jar

Adjustable spanners:

These also come in a profusion of shapes and sizes. A 6-inch or 8-inch one of the type illustrated will be found quite useful. The Mole wrench is also a good tool because it can be locked on the job.

Further equipment:

A wirebrush is handy for cleaning away rust and dirt. A funnel will be needed for brake fluid. The best type of tyre pump is operated by the foot and it saves time if it carries its own pressure gauge. Alternatively, use the push-on type illustrated. The 12-volt inspection lamp will be invaluable in the dark and may also be used for test purposes. It may be run off the battery. Insulating tape is available in the original sticky black variety, but the modern plastic kind is probably the best buy.

2:4 The stores

There is an infinite list of useful stores that we could recommend you to provide, but most owners are content to make gradual acquisitions. However, it is a good plan to buy your oil in bulk because it will certainly keep down the cost of motoring.

A can of brake fluid will be needed. Check with the maker's recommendation in **Facts and Figures** before making your purchase. **Do not keep brake fluid in an open jar.**

Any good make of multi-purpose grease will be suitable for use in the grease-gun.

There will be a constant need for distilled water for the battery. In an emergency it is possible to use the water that is collected when a refrigerator is defrosted.

So far as mechanical spares are concerned, it is useful to keep a set of new sparking plugs, a new rocker cover gasket, a spare belt and a few spare bulbs of appropriate sizes.

2:5 Testing after carrying out repairs

When you have completed a job on the car, particularly after working on the brakes or steering, it is advisable to approach the problem of testing with care.

Before taking the car on the road, go over all the jobs in retrospect and check everything you have done. Apply heavy pressure to the brake pedal and get a second person to check every possible source of hydraulic leakage. The brakes may seem to work well, but a leak could cause complete failure after a few miles (see **Section 6:10**). The same applies to oil leakage after draining the sump and renewing the oil filter.

Do not fit the hub discs until every wheel nut has been checked for tightness. Check tyre pressures and the levels of water, oil and brake fluid. If you are satisfied that all is well, take the car on the road and test the footbrake at once. Check the steering and the handbrake. Do all tests at a moderate speed and make sure there is no other vehicle behind you if you are going to carry out a braking test.

DAY TO DAY RUNNING

3:1 Keys and locks

The locks are not marked with the key numbers, so make a note of the numbers and keep them in a safe place, **but not in the car.** Buy a duplicate ignition key and fasten it to the car where it cannot be seen but where it is accessible if you lose your key and the car is locked. A magnetic key-holder is available that will adhere to any steel part of the car.

On some models there is a key-operated switch and lock on the steering column (see **FIG 1:19** in **Chapter 1**). In one type, to lock the steering, turn the key to **1** and either press the key inwards or press the button (see arrow, top right), turn the key to **0** and withdraw it. On other models, turn the key back to **0** and withdraw it. When the steering wheel is turned the lock will 'click' into engagement.

The rear doors on the early four-door models can be locked by pushing down the inside operating lever. The levers on the front doors return to their neutral position after they have been pushed down. Because of this, the locks will operate only when the doors are shut. The last door from which an exit is made must then be locked on the outside with the key.

Anti-burst type locks have been incorporated in later two-door models (see **FIG 3:2**). To lock the doors from the inside, the latch is pushed rearwards, but as it can be moved only when the doors are shut, the last door used for exit must be locked from the outside.

To lock doors on the outside, turn the top of the key towards the front of the car (see **FIG 3:1**).

Child safety locks:

To prevent the doors from being opened by children on the inside, a safety trip is fitted to some door locks When the lever shown in **FIG 3:1** is switched to the 'ON' position the interior lever is made inoperative and the door can be opened only from the outside. Locking the door with the large interior lever is not affected.

3:2 Lifting the bonnet

To unlock the bonnet on the MG, Princess, Riley and Wolseley a remote control knob is provided on the righthand side, below the facia panel. The bonnet will spring upwards when the knob is pulled and will then be checked by a safety catch (see inset in **FIG 3:3**). From the front of the car, release the safety catch by pushing it in the direction indicated by the arrow. It may be necessary to press down gently on top of the bonnet to do this. Lift the bonnet until the stay-locking lever automatically engages (see **FIG 3:4**).

On Austin and Morris models there is a different arrangement. As you will see in **FIG 3:3**, the release lever is positioned between the upper slats of the front grille. Press down on the bonnet and at the same time push the release lever to the left. The bonnet will spring up slightly. Push the safety catch to the right. If it is held by the bonnet, press down slightly to release it. Lift and prop the bonnet as just described.

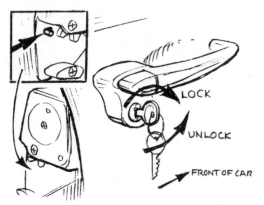

FIG 3:1 How to lock and unlock the front doors with the ignition key. Inset shows location of child-proof locking lever

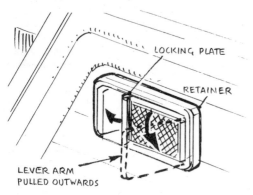

FIG 3:2 Interior door control on later 2-door models. Lever is pulled out to open door when locking plate is right forward. Move plate to rear to lock door

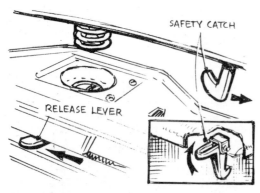

FIG 3:3 Releasing the bonnet on Austin/Morris cars. First move the release lever, then trip the safety catch to the right. All other models have a release knob inside the car and a safety catch lever that must be lifted (see inset)

To close the bonnet, lift it slightly and push on the stay locking catch to release it (see **FIG 3:4**). Lower the bonnet and apply two-handed pressure to lock it.

3:3 Boot lid and window locks

On saloon cars the boot lid is unlocked as shown in **FIG 3:5**. Press the button to release the catch. The catches for the sliding windows on Traveller and Countryman models are shown in **FIG 3:6**.

3:4 Cleaning the car
The inside:

Brush carpets with a stiff brush or use a vacuum cleaner. Battery-operated cleaners are available for cars. Clean the rubber matting with a damp cloth. Soiled carpets, upholstery and roof lining may be cleaned with Decosol or similar interior cleaner.

The outside:

To wash the car it is preferable to use a brush on the end of a hose. A foam sponge and a chamois leather will also be needed. If a hose is not available use a bucket and several changes of water.

Soak the dirt with a soft jet of water. Keep the windows closed. A strong jet will remove caked mud from underneath. Do this frequently in winter if salt has been used on icy roads. After spraying water in the region of the brakes, take care to check them at once when driving. Wet brakes may be ineffective and must be dried off by repeated applications.

Soaked dirt must be lifted off the panels with a sponge and plenty of water. Do not scrub the dirt around or it will scour the paintwork. A shampoo may be used to remove grime and prepare the paintwork for a final polish after drying off with the chamois leather. It is best not to clean and polish the car in full sun. Drops of water act as lenses and may cause paint discolouration if bright sunshine is allowed to dry them off.

Never touch the windscreen glass with any of the cleaning cloths, as the silicone content of most polishes may be transferred to the glass and make effective screen-wiping in wet weather impossible (see **Section 3:6**).

3:5 Polishing the car

Frequent wax-polishing of the car is unnecessary. Two or three applications a year is all that is required, especially when using silicone polishes. New cars or re-enamelled bodies should not be polished at all for the first few weeks to allow the paint to harden. Neglected paintwork on older cars may need an abrasive cleaner and polisher. Many of the polishes combine an abrasive cleaner and can be obtained in liquid or paste form.

Do not use these abrasive cleaners on the chrome-plated parts. If they have become tarnished use BMC Chrome Cleaner to restore the shine.

3:6 Cleaning windows and windscreens

It is wise to take the greatest care not to get silicone-wax polish on the windscreen. This usually happens when the screen is cleaned with a duster that has been used on the paintwork. The result is a disastrous smeariness that the wiper blades cannot clear even when the screen washer is used.

If such smeariness is apparent, clean off any dirt and then use methylated spirit, household ammonia or one of the windscreen cleaners sold for the purpose. To reach all the glass, pull the wiper blades outwards against the pressure of the springs.

3:7 Commonsense methods of routine maintenance

For the owner who prefers to follow the maker's recommendations, full instructions will be found in **Chapters 5** and **6**. We find, from experience, that very few owners slavishly follow the short-term checking and this Section is devoted to suggestions for reasonable checking intervals.

Much, of course, depends on the age and condition of the car. Obviously a new car is going to need less frequent checking than an elderly model that has a leak in its water system and a worn engine that is thirsty for oil.

In addition to the general instructions we have included some advice on the avoidance of bad driving habits that may prove costly.

After making the following short-term checks it is recommended that you follow the makers schedules for greater mileages, starting with **Chapter 5, Section 5:3.**

3:8 Checking levels of oil and water

If you have just bought a secondhand car, make frequent checks at first until you have found out whether there is anything unusual about the consumption of oil and water. The need for frequent topping up will show that something is wrong and you will then find the checks in **Solve-it-yourself** most useful.

From your initial checks on a new or used car you will soon establish reasonable checking intervals. As it is likely that most owners will find it unnecessary to make daily checks, we suggest that you get into the habit of making them at convenient times. These may be when you are at a filling station or when you are waiting for passengers. If you wipe the radiator filler cap, the dipstick handle and the battery filler plugs you will be able to do the checking in your ordinary clothes and without making your hands dirty.

Checking should be done when the car is standing reasonably level.

FIG 3:4 The bonnet stay automatically props it in the open position. To close bonnet lift it slightly and operate the safety catch in direction of arrow

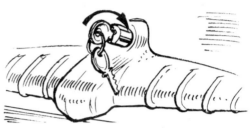

FIG 3:5 Use separate key (not ignition key) to lock luggage compartment. Open lid by depressing button

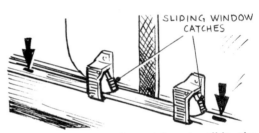

FIG 3:6 Depress the catches to slide the windows on Countryman and Traveller cars. Engage the catch plungers in the holes indicated to lock the windows

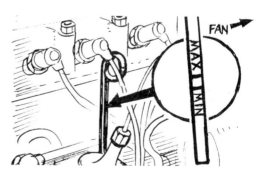

FIG 3:7 The oil dipstick is centrally located in front of the engine on cars with the normal hand gearchange. Inset shows markings

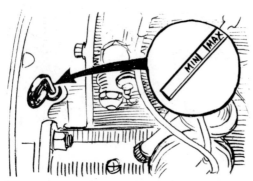

FIG 3:8 On cars with automatic transmission the engine dipstick is low down on the left (facing the engine). Inset shows markings

FIG 3:9 There is every chance of severe scalding if you remove the filler cap from the radiator after using the car on the road. Note that cap is quite plain. Cap for expansion tank has a spring-loaded valve (see below)

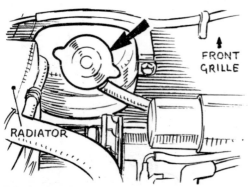

FIG 3:10 The expansion chamber takes overflow from the radiator. It is mounted low down under the front valance. Do not remove the cap, but see also Chapter 5

Checking the oil level:

On cars with manual transmission, this should be done when the engine is cold. If the car has automatic transmission, do it when the engine is hot.

To check the level just after the engine has been running wipe the dipstick clean and reinsert it to find the correct level. It is important to make quite sure that you have pushed the dipstick downwards to its fullest extent.

See **FIGS 3:7** and **3:8** for the location of the dipstick. The oil will need topping up if the level has dropped to the MIN (minimum) mark. **Do not let the level drop below this.** When topping up, try to avoid filling above the MAX (maximum) mark (see **Chapter 5**).

Engines with manual transmission take about one pint of oil to span the marks. The filler cap is shown in **3:19**.

Checking the water level in the radiator:

Check this when the engine is cold. **Do not remove the cap when the engine is hot or severe scalding may result (see FIG 3:9).** The location of the cap is shown in **FIG 3:19**.

To remove it, turn the cap anticlockwise. The correct coolant level is to the bottom edge of the filler neck. In winter, use antifreeze solution when topping up to prevent the dilution that would otherwise lower the degree of protection. Do not interfere with the expansion tank cap shown in **FIG 3:10** but see **Section 5:3 (3)** in **Chapter 5**.

3:9 Checking the battery

Topping up with distilled water is necessary when the level of the battery electrolyte (acid) has dropped below the top of the internal parts. If you cannot see the reflecting surface of the liquid it is time to add distilled water.

Dispensers that release the correct volume of electrolyte are available in accessory shops. The required level is $\frac{1}{8}$ inch above the internal plates. Do not overfill or there may be trouble with acid leakage and corrosion.

Topping up intervals depend on battery use and weather, heat causing increased evaporation. A battery might need topping up once a week or as infrequently as once a month. Make your own assessment by watching it closely for a period. To check, lift off the filler manifold or unscrew the six caps. Refer to **Chapter 5** for instructions on topping up and battery care. **Never use a naked flame near battery cells, as inflammable gas may be present.**

3:10 Checking tyre pressure and tread pattern

Pressures should be checked every week, especially if one tyre seems to lose pressure more rapidly than the others. An under-inflated tyre wears out faster and the sidewalls may be damaged.

Check when the tyres are cold as a hot tyre will give a higher reading. Correct pressures are quoted in **Facts and Figures**. Do not forget to check the spare wheel (see **FIG 3:12**).

To use the tyre gauge, remove the dust cap and press the head of the gauge firmly onto the valve. Do not worry about the initial hiss of escaping air. Make sure the gauge plunger is pushed fully in before use.

The plunger will be pushed out by air pressure. Remove the gauge and read the figure at the line nearest to the end of the gauge housing (see **FIG 3:11**).

Walk round the car and check the tread pattern for excessive or unusual wear. **Section 4:27** in **Chapter 4** will tell you about the characteristics.

At one time it was considered good practice to move wheels to new positions to equalize tyre wear. This is no longer recommended, particularly if you have had the wheel assemblies balanced while mounted on the hubs. Fitting a wheel to a different hub may upset the original balancing and this may lead to trouble with vibration and uneven tyre wear. Another important point is that equalizing tyre wear means that you have to buy a complete set of new tyres all at once!

It will be found that the rear tyres will last twice as long as the front because the front tyres have to steer and drive.

Three types of tyre are available, and these are known as cross-ply, radial-ply and bias-belted. It is dangerous to mix different types on the front and rear, and safest to use one type all round, including the spare. Further amplification of this warning will be found in **Chapter 4, Section 4:26**.

3:11 The type of fuel to use

Three-star (94-96 octane) fuel is recommended for low-compression engines and four-star (97-99 octane) for high-compression engines. To find out what type of engine is fitted in your car so that the correct grade can be used, look at the engine number (see **FIG 1:7**). The letter immediately preceding the last group of numbers will be either an L (low) or H (high). It is unnecessary expense to use a higher grade of fuel than the one recommended.

3:12 Combating the effects of damp, frost and snow

If your car is parked outside it may be difficult to start in the winter months due to damp on the distributor and spark plugs. You will find **Chapter 7** very helpful in tracing and curing such faults.

Frozen snow or frost can be readily removed from the windscreen and windows with de-icing fluid supplied in aerosol spray cans. Plastic scrapers will also do the job.

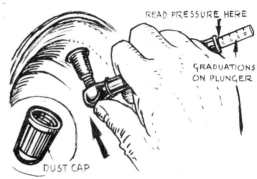

FIG 3:11 When checking tyre pressures, press the gauge firmly into place on the valve. Always refit the cap (left). It forms a second seal and excludes dirt

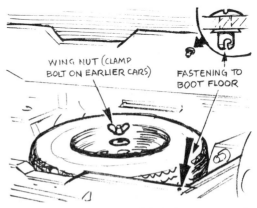

FIG 3:12 On most models it is necessary to remove the spare wheel in order to check the pressure or inflate the tyre. The boot floor may have press-type fasteners or, on later models, the locking type shown (top right)

FIG 3:13 Most models have front seat adjustment as shown above. Lift the lever and slide the seat to the required position. The inset shows how to extend the range by moving the brackets

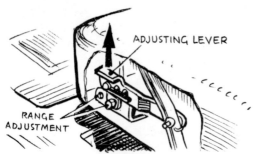

FIG 3:14 Later 1100/1300 models have a modified form of front seat adjustment. Additional range is provided at the anchorage brackets

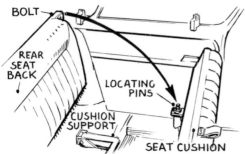

FIG 3:15 On Countryman and Traveller models, extra floor space is obtained by folding down the rear seat back after lifting the seat cushion

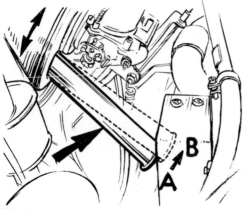

FIG 3:16 On early cars with manual gear-change, position the intake to the air cleaner at A in the winter and B in the summer

Instructions on how to add antifreeze to the cooling system are given in **Chapter 6**. Keep the windscreen washer container filled with water and the correct type of de-icing fluid. **Do not put radiator antifreeze into the container as this will smear the windscreen and damage the paintwork.** The location of the washer bottle is shown in **FIG 3:19**. Make sure the central tube reaches well down into the bottle. Blocked jets may be cleared with fine wire.

3:13 Seat adjustment

The front seat position is adjustable and is locked by a spring-loaded lever (see **FIG 3:13**). To adjust, lift the lever and slide the seat to a comfortable position. Lock it by releasing the lever. The seat may have to be moved slightly until the lever clicks into position.

The adjustment range can be extended by altering the positions of the pivot brackets (see inset). Use the pair of holes in the floor that gives best results. It is also possible to turn the brackets to point to the rear, giving a more comfortable position for drivers with long legs. Later models have alternative positions in the brackets (see **FIG 3:14**).

The seat backs on later models can be adjusted for rake by lifting the locking handle. They can be lowered fully for sleeping. Push the lever down to hold the squab in the desired position. On Vanden Plas models the angle of the seat back may be adjusted by turning a handle on the front face of the seat assembly.

Countryman and Traveller:

To increase the luggage compartment space the rear seat and back-rest can be folded away. Look at **FIG 3:15** and then withdraw the sliding bolts at the rear of the back seat. Pull the back-rest slightly forward to make the bolts move easily. Let the back-rest hinge rearwards until it rests on the floor. Lift the rear edge of the seat cushion, bringing it forward until it is vertical. Check that the seat cushion support on the floor of the car is in the lowered position as shown in the illustration. Swing the back-rest right over and fit the back-rest brackets over the pins on the seat brackets. Follow the curved arrow.

To provide sleeping accommodation on Countryman and Traveller cars, pull the front seats fully forward. Push the back of the rear seat forward to clear the bolts from the body. Withdraw the bolts and lie the back-rest flat on the floor behind. Lift the rear edge of the seat cushion, erect the support, and rest the seat on it. The front seat back is then lowered to the reclining position.

3:14 Sliding roof operation

Your Vanden Plas Princess may have a sliding roof. To open the roof, pull the operating handle down-wards and turn it anticlockwise.

3:15 The danger of wet brakes

After the car has been washed with a hose or driven through a watersplash, the brakes may be wet and completely ineffective. It is a good plan to check them at once and if they have obviously lost most of their stopping power, drive slowly and keep applying them until they have dried out.

3:16 Fitting seat belts

If your car is not fitted with seat belts, do not fit them yourself but obtain the services of a garage or a skilled mechanic. **Your life may depend on the security of the belts, so please make sure that they are correctly installed.**

3:17 Position of air intake in summer and winter

On all models the intake to the air cleaner may be set for summer or winter conditions. By moving the intake nearer to the exhaust manifold, heated air enters the carburetter to prevent icing-up in very cold weather.

On early cars, slacken the air cleaner wingnut and turn the intake to position A in winter and B in summer as shown in **FIG 3:16**. Tighten the wingnut afterwards.

On later cars, slacken the clip shown in **FIG 3:17**. The positions are the same as those for earlier cars.

On later MG and other twin-carburetter models there is a sliding intake that is positioned after the clip is slackened (see **FIG 3:18**).

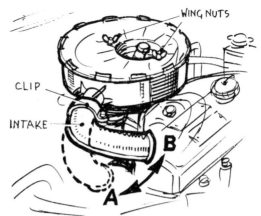

FIG 3:17 On 1300, on early twin-carburetter, and all automatic transmission models position intake to air cleaner at A in winter and at B in summer

FIG 3:18 On later twin-carburetter models position the intake to the air cleaner at A in winter and B in summer

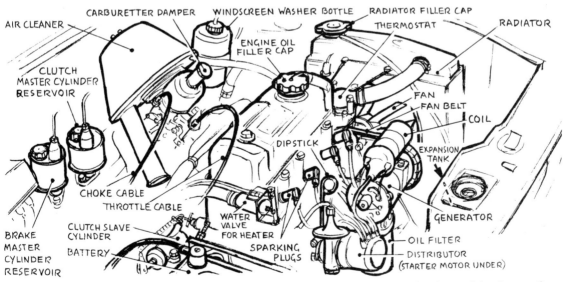

FIG 3:19 A typical under-bonnet view showing the location of parts referred to in servicing instructions

3:18 Driving habits that may prove expensive

A habit that leads to a lot of trouble with a car is furious driving. Fierce acceleration, crash-braking, and high-speed cornering will take their toll. In addition, fuel costs will rise if the car is driven to the limit all the time. The effect on the tyres may well be disastrous.

Rapid clutch wear may result from excessive slipping in order to make a rapid start with a fast-revving engine. It may also result from slipping the clutch in an effort to climb steep hills without changing down to a lower gear. The clutch-operating mechanism wears out faster if the left foot is allowed to rest on the pedal when the clutch is fully engaged.

Excessive engine wear may be attributable to leaving the choke knob pulled out too long after the engine has started. Excess fuel washes the oil off the cylinder walls. Push the choke knob in as quickly as possible after starting. It may be left in the fast-idle position without harm (see **Chapter 4, Section 4:4**). This is when the control knob is pulled out about $\frac{1}{2}$ inch.

Using cheap oil may be costly:

The engine and transmission have highly-stressed working parts that need the best lubrication they can be given. Always use the recommended oils. Trying to cut the cost of motoring by using cheap oil may prove expensive if it leads to mechanical failure.

3:19 Regular care pays dividends

This chapter has covered most of the servicing that is needed to keep your car running from day to day. The following chapters are devoted to the servic-ing requirements after higher mileages or long periods of time have elapsed. It must, of course, be emphasized that even the most thorough servicing likely to fail if the car is in poor mechanical condition. If your car has covered a very high mileage, or ha obviously been neglected by a previous owner, it essential to have the faults rectified before use servicing can have the desired effect.

With your car in good mechanical condition regular servicing will help enormously in keeping that way. There is the added advantage that you w become familiar with the basic equipment and location, and this knowledge may be particular useful if you are unfortunate enough to have troub on the road.

It will be appreciated that a highly-complex pie of engineering such as a modern car may sometim fail in spite of regular and painstaking servicing.

If this should happen to you, we suggest th reading **Chapter 7** will start you off on the rig lines if you propose to tackle the problem yourse Long experience may enable you to pinpoint t trouble quickly, but the logical sequence of tes laid out in that chapter will ensure that a les experienced owner will be able to trace the defe in much less time than would be spent in haphaza searches.

Try to make your servicing pay dividends by kee your eyes open for any untoward happening und the bonnet. A quick glance may reveal a frayed be or a detached wire in time to prevent a roadsic breakdown.

Use **FIG 3:19** to familiarise yourself with t components under the bonnet. This will simpli your servicing.

TUNING AND ADJUSTMENT

:1 The meaning of 'tuning'

To 'tune' an engine it is necessary to establish a tate of harmony between the three main factors, arburation, ignition, and the mechanical condition f the engine. Like a good orchestra, these parts must ll be playing the same tune at the right strength and t the right time!

The carburation system produces a petrol/air ixture of the correct proportions at all engine speeds. here are adjustments for this.

The ignition, through the battery, coil, distributor nd sparking plugs will ignite the petrol/air mixture t the right time. The moment of ignition may also e adjusted.

The mechanical condition and adjustment of the ngine will affect the two preceding factors. **A worn ngine will make accurate tuning impossible.** part from adjusting the valve clearance there is othing else to be done about mechanical condition, nd a worn engine must be reconditioned. If the car as covered a high mileage it may be a good thing o have the engine decarbonized and the valves erviced before spending too much time on tuning.

4:2 When to tune

Many of our readers will own secondhand cars and these may be quite out of tune. Knowing the correct state of tune is not always easy for an inexperienced owner. In this case it is a good idea to enlist the aid of a knowledgeable friend or competent garage mechanic. He will be able to comment on your car and tell you what he thinks is wrong with it.

Without his help you must make such adjustments as you think are necessary. The logical way to solve problems is to read **Chapter 7** first. The **Solve-it-yourself** method of pinpointing the cure for particular defects will be found invaluable. If there is nothing obviously wrong with the way your engine is running the sensible plan is to leave well alone!

THE FUEL SYSTEM

4:3 When to tune the carburetter

The carburetter may be out of tune if the engine will not idle smoothly, if it stops unexpectedly, if engine performance is down or if petrol consumption is excessive. Petrol/air mixture strength may be wrong, giving rise to 'rich' or 'weak' mixture.

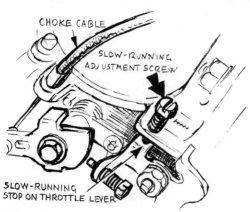

CHOKE CABLE
SLOW-RUNNING ADJUSTMENT SCREW
SLOW-RUNNING STOP ON THROTTLE LEVER

FIG 4:1 Location of the carburetter slow-running adjustment screw. Lower end of screw contacts stop on throttle lever

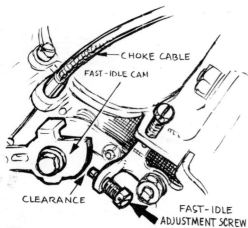

CHOKE CABLE
FAST-IDLE CAM
CLEARANCE
FAST-IDLE ADJUSTMENT SCREW

FIG 4:2 Location of the carburetter fast-idle adjustment screw. Note the clearance when the throttle is closed and the choke control is pushed right in

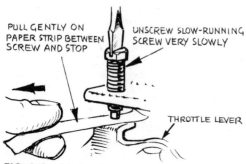

PULL GENTLY ON PAPER STRIP BETWEEN SCREW AND STOP
UNSCREW SLOW-RUNNING SCREW VERY SLOWLY
THROTTLE LEVER

FIG 4:3 A simple method of determining when the slow-running screw loses contact with the throttle lever stop

If it is too rich there is too much petrol for the volume of air entering the engine. This may be recognised by black smoke from the exhaust pipe and a strong smell of petrol. The engine will idle with a soft regular thump exactly like the sound you get if you leave the choke control pulled out too long after starting (see **FIG 4 : 20**).

Weak mixture causes irregular firing and, if severe, a tendency for the engine to stop at idling speeds (see **FIG 4 : 20**).

It is advisable to re-tune the carburetter after the engine of a new car is properly run-in.

Before tuning the carburetter:

First check that any defect in engine performance is not due to one of the interdependent factors. These are:

1 The contact breaker points gap (see **Section 4 : 9**).
2 The ignition timing (see **Section 4 : 10**).
3 Sparking plug condition and gap adjustment (see **Section 4 : 11**).
4 Valve clearances (see **Section 4 : 14**).
5 Cleanliness of air filter (see **Chapter 6, Section 6 : 3**).
6 That the carburetter piston is not sticking (see **Section 4 : 6**).
7 That the carburetter jet needle is correctly fitted to the piston and that it is the needle recommended by the manufacturers. The correct needle is listed in **Facts and Figures.**

A new car will have the correct needle. On a secondhand car, amateur tuning may have resulted in the wrong needle being fitted. If your own tuning does not give the desired results and the ignition and mechanical details are known to be correct, then have the needle checked by a service station. **Do not simply fit a new needle, as this is less than half the job. Any disturbance of a needle calls for centralizing of the jet and this is an exacting operation that is best left to the experts.**

Cars with manual transmission have either a single or twin SU.HS2 carburetter and models with automatic transmission are fitted with either a single or twin HS4's. Although both types of carburetter work on the same principle, the HS4 cannot be tuned without a tachometer or revolution indicator, as the idling speed must be set accurately to ensure smooth gear changes. Models that are not fitted with a tachometer should be taken to a garage for tuning. Special instructions for tuning the twin carburetter versions are given in **Section 4 : 7.**

4:4 Tuning the single carburetter

Idling speed setting:

1 Start the engine and run it up to normal operating temperature. If the car is fitted with automatic transmission the selector must be in the 'N' position and the handbrake applied.

2 **FIGS 4:1** and **4:2** show the idling adjustment screws. Push the choke knob right in and check that the fast-idling screw is not touching its operating cam. If it is, unscrew it until it is just clear (see **FIG 4:2**). With the engine idling, turn the throttle adjusting screw slowly in and out. Screwing it in will increase engine speed and unscrewing it will slow it down. When the screw is fully unscrewed clear of the stop, the engine may stop.

3 To adjust to the correct idling speed, undo the screw until it is just clear of the stop. Turn the screw fractionally inwards until it just touches the stop, then turn it a further one and a half turns. Check the tachometer reading on models with automatic transmission and, if necessary, adjust the screw to give a reading of 650 rev/min. There is a useful tip about setting the screw and stop which is made clear in **FIG 4:3**.

Slow-running mixture setting:

4 Leave the engine ticking over and refer to **FIGS 4:4** and **4:5** for the location of the jet adjusting nut. This nut adjusts the mixture strength. To obtain the correct setting, start with a rich mixture and gradually reduce it until the correct mixture is obtained (see **FIG 4:5**). Use a spanner if you cannot turn the nut with your fingers. There is a special SU spanner made for the job, but a short open-ended spanner may be used instead. Turn the nut slowly downwards, or clockwise when viewed from above. The mixture will get richer and the engine will begin to run 'heavily' (see **Section 4:3**).

5 When this happens, screw the nut in the opposite direction, a fraction of a turn each time. Keep one finger on the bottom of the jet and press upwards to ensure that the jet head is kept against the face of the nut (see **FIG 4:6**).

Listen to the 'beat' of the engine. Try to obtain the fastest idling speed without any misfiring or staggering. When you are satisfied that you have the best setting and the smoothest running, it may be necessary to reduce the speed by using the idling adjustment screw. If the car has automatic transmission, adjust to an idling speed of 650 rev/min. Leave the engine ticking over and again check the mixture setting, moving the adjusting nut only fractionally this time. When satisfied with the smooth running of the engine, make a final slight adjustment to the idling speed if required.

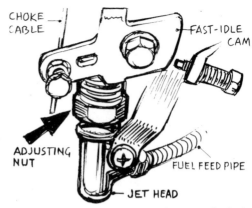

FIG 4:4 Look under the carburetter body to find the mixture adjusting nut

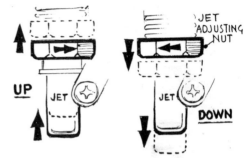

FIG 4:5 How the strength of the petrol/air mixture is modified by turning the adjusting nut

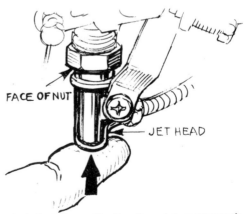

FIG 4:6 When adjusting the mixture strength, always press upwards on the jet head to ensure that it makes contact with the face of the nut

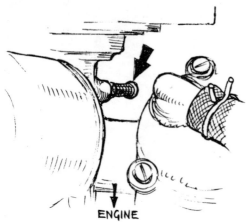

FIG 4:7 The carburetter piston lifting pin is low down behind the float chamber

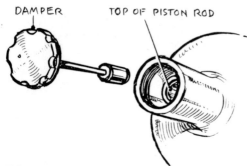

FIG 4:8 When the damper is unscrewed from the carburetter suction chamber the top end of the piston rod is visible

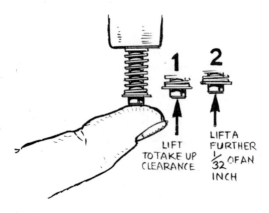

FIG 4:9 The two stages of operating the piston lifting pin

Checking the mixture setting:

6 The setting must now be checked to find out if the mixture is correct. Refer to **FIG 4:7** to locate the piston lifting pin. You can just get your hand behind the float chamber to place one finger on the pin. Unscrew and remove the damper (see **FIG 4:8**).

7 Raise the lifting pin and take up the free movement before it touches the piston (see **FIG 4:9**). As you lift the piston you will see the piston rod moving inside the damper orifice. Try to judge the lift by watching the rod (see **FIG 4:8**).

8 When you are satisfied that the pin is touching the piston, lift the piston a further $\frac{1}{32}$ of an inch (see **FIG 4:9**). This is nearly the diameter of a pin's head. Watch the piston rod to check the movement. While you are doing this, the engine will do one of three things:

(a) Increase speed and continue to pick-up, in which case **the mixture is too rich.**

(b) Immediately decrease speed because **the mixture is too weak.**

(c) Increase speed momentarily and then continue to run smoothly. **The mixture is correct.**

If you have condition (a) or (b), adjust the nut again, one flat at a time, richening or weakening the mixture until the correct balance is obtained as in (c).

Resetting the fast idling:

The fast-idling screw and cam are needed to give a higher engine speed for starting from cold. They come into action when the choke knob is pulled out. Adjust as follows:

1 After completing the mixture setting adjustments, the fast-idle adjustment must be reset. Switch off the engine and refer to **FIG 4:10**. Select a 15 thousandths of an inch feeler gauge and adjust the fast idling screw so that the gauge just slides between the screw and the cam. Remove the feeler.

2 Check the adjustment by starting the engine and pulling out the choke knob between $\frac{1}{4}$ and $\frac{1}{2}$ an inch (this is the fast idling position). This initial movement turns the cam, opens the throttle without operating the choke, and gives a fast idling speed.

3 On cars with automatic transmission, check that the tachometer reading is 1050 rev/min. If it is not, adjust the fast idling and recheck the slow idling.

4:5 Flooding of the carburetter

The supply of fuel to the carburetter jet is controlled by the maintenance of a constant level in the float chamber. This is done with a float and a needle valve. The float chamber is shown in **FIG 4:11**.

Carburetter flooding is due to a fault in the valve or the float. Usually it is due to a worn needle or seating. Dirt may also cause the needle to stick in the 'open' position. Flooding can often be detected by a strong smell of petrol inside the car and a high fuel consumption. Flooding will only occur when the ignition is switched on because it is only then that the electric fuel pump is working.

To check for flooding, lift the bonnet and switch on the ignition. **Take precautions against an accidental fire.** If there is a fault in the float chamber, petrol will overflow and spill round the outside. Switch off the ignition.

Removing the float chamber cover:

1 Refer to **FIG 4:11**. To remove the feed pipe, compress the ends of the clip with a pair of pliers and pull off the hose.
2 Remove the three screws and washers securing the cover. You may have difficulty with the rear screw because of its proximity to the air filter. If so, refer to **Chapter 6, Section 6:3** and remove the filter and casing.
3 Lift off the cover, with the attached float and needle valve (see **FIG 4:12**). The float chamber can be cleaned by soaking out the petrol with kitchen paper or a non-fluffy rag. **Make sure no fluff from rag or paper is left behind.**

Removing the needle valve:

4 Extract the float hinge pin with a pair of pliers. Grip the pin at the serrated end after giving a light tap at the other end.
5 Check the float for punctures by shaking it. This will reveal the presence of fuel inside. Fit a new float if the test indicates a puncture.
6 Lift the needle and examine the conical end for wear. This will be in the form of a groove and may need a magnifying glass for positive identification. If there is any doubt, and if the car has covered a considerable mileage it is wise to renew the needle assembly. Spares are available at British Leyland service stations. A box spanner is needed to unscrew the housing.

Reassembling the float chamber:

7 Insert the needle valve, taper end first. Fit the float and insert the hinge pin, plain end first. Tap the pin lightly home.

Checking the float setting:

8 Turn the cover with the float uppermost as shown in **FIG 4:13**. The needle valve will then be closed.
9 Place a $\frac{5}{32}$ inch bar or drill across the **centre** of the cover. The face of the float lever should just rest on the bar. If it is not more than $\frac{1}{32}$ of an inch out

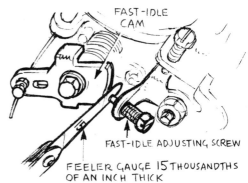

FIG 4:10 Setting the fast-idling speed with the choke control fully closed

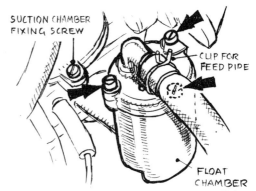

FIG 4:11 The arrows point to the three fixing screws for the float chamber cover

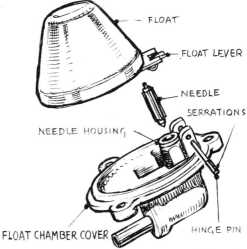

FIG 4:12 The separate parts comprising the float chamber cover assembly

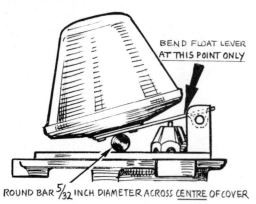

ROUND BAR 5/32 INCH DIAMETER ACROSS CENTRE OF COVER

FIG 4:13 Using a piece of round bar to check float lever setting

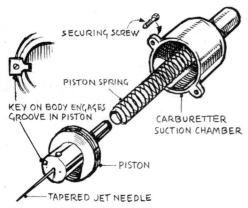

FIG 4:14 The carburetter piston and suction chamber assembly. Note how piston is prevented from turning by a key (top left)

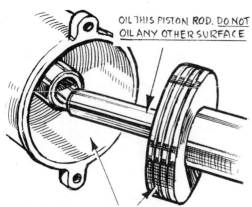

FIG 4:15 Dirt in the suction chamber and on the piston rim may cause piston to stick. Note instruction about lubrication

either way do not worry about it. If it is more than this the float lever must be bent with thin-nosed pliers at the point shown. **Do not bend the lever at any other point.**

Refitting the float cover:

10 Check that the cover gasket is sound. Refit the cover.
11 Compress the ends of the clip, refit the hose and release the clip.
12 Switch on the ignition and check for leaks. The hose may leak because the spring clip has lost its tension. Renew the clip or fit a small screw-operated hose clip.

4:6 Removing the suction chamber and piston

A sticking piston is frequently indicated by difficult starting and lack of response to the accelerator pedal. To check piston freedom, remove the damper (see **FIG 4:8**). With the lifting pin (see **FIG 4:7**) lift the piston and then let it fall freely. It should drop smartly and with an audible click as it comes to rest. If it is sluggish, the suction chamber and piston should be removed for cleaning. It is also possible that the needle may be bent.

1 Refer to **FIG 4:14** and remove the two screws that secure the suction chamber. Mark the body and the chamber with a scratch for refitting in the original position. **Exercise the greatest care during the next operation. Any damage to the parts may make matters worse.** Note that there is a spring inside the chamber.
2 Carefully ease off the chamber. As it is pulled upwards the piston will be exposed. Hold the piston and chamber together and lift the assembly, keeping it straight to avoid bending the needle. Pour out the oil from the damper chamber.
3 Separate the parts. The spring will be red in a single carburetter and blue in twin carburetters.
4 Clean the chamber and piston thoroughly with petrol and a non-fluffy rag.
5 **The piston rim must not touch the inside of the chamber** (see **FIG 4:15**). Lightly oil the piston rod and insert it into the chamber. Hold the assembly horizontally and spin the piston inside the chamber to ensure that it is not touching anywhere. Also check that the needle runs true. **Do not drop the piston, otherwise it will mean renewing the piston, the chamber and possibly the needle.** If the piston touches the inside of the chamber, the assembly may need renewal. Get a second opinion from a service station, particularly if a bent needle is suspected.
6 Refit the assembly. Take care as you insert the needle and make sure the groove in the piston engages the key in the body (see **FIG 4:14**).

7 **Do not oil the inside of the chamber or the piston.** The only part to be lubricated is the steel piston rod (see **FIG 4:15**). Fit the spring in the chamber large end first (see **FIG 4:16**). Fit the chamber and align the marks. Refit the screws.

Check the movement of the piston by referring to the test at the beginning of this Section. Put engine oil in the dashpot (see **Chapter 5**) and refit the damper.

4:7 Tuning twin carburetters

This operation needs time, patience and concentration, with no distracting noises. If after reading the following instructions, you doubt your ability to make a success of the operation, entrust it to a specialist service station.

Before the actual tuning is tackled the carburetters must be synchronized as follows:

Synchronizing and slow-running adjustment:

1 Run the engine up to normal working temperature. **This is important.** Switch off and remove the air cleaner elements (see **Chapter 6, Section 6:3**). Release the air cleaner intake pipes from the carburetter flanges. Detach the hose (if fitted) from the rocker cover.

2 Refer to **FIGS 4:21** and **4:22** according to model. Slacken the throttle shaft lever clamping bolts. Turn back the throttle adjusting screws so that their lower ends are clear of the stops on the carburetter levers. Insert a strip of very thin paper between screw and stop and turn the screws downwards until the paper is just nipped (see **FIG 4:3**). Remove the paper and continue to turn the screws downwards or clockwise by one full turn. The position of the screwdriver slot will act as an indicator. Both throttles will now be open by an equal amount.

3 Remove the suction chambers and pistons as in **Section 4:6** for single-carburetter installations. Follow the instructions for cleaning and checking. Remove the choke control cable (see **FIG 4:23**), but first make a note of the length of cable sticking out below the clamp. It will then be possible to reconnect it in the same position (see **FIG 4:17**).

4 If you look down inside the carburetter bodies from the suction chamber flange you will see the brass jet tubes that take the piston needles (see **FIG 4:18**). These tubes may be raised or lowered by turning the adjusting nuts (see **FIG 4:4**). Set both of them as level as possible with the flat bridges across the floors of the intakes (see **FIG 4:18**). Get both tubes into identical positions if possible, keeping the jet heads pressed upwards from below. Refit the suction chambers and pistons as in operations 6 and 7 in **Section 4:6** but do not fit the damper. Insert a finger in

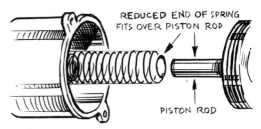

FIG 4:16 The piston spring has one end reduced in diameter. Make sure that it is correctly fitted

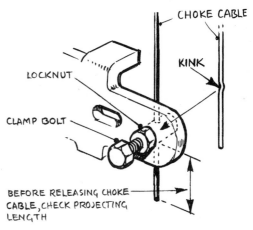

FIG 4:17 Before disconnecting the choke control cable from the lever clamp, make a note of the length of wire projecting. The kink (top right) is also a useful indication of position

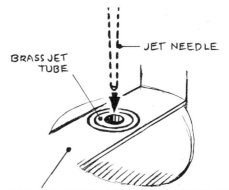

FIG 4:18 When synchronizing twin carburetters, set the jet tubes as level as possible with the bridges across the carburetter intake bores

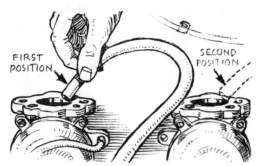

FIG 4:19 Using a piece of tubing to compare the hiss at twin carburetter intakes. The positions must be the same

RICH MIXTURE - BLACK SMOKE, REGULAR BEAT

WEAK MIXTURE - CLEAR EXHAUST, IRREGULAR BEAT

FIG 4:20 The colour and beat of the exhaust will give some clue to the adjustment of the carburetter system

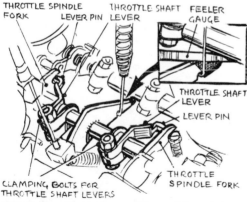

FIG 4:21 On engines with an 8.8 to 1 compression ratio and twin carburetters, set the throttle shaft clearance at the point indicated by the arrow

each carburetter intake and lift the pistons. They should fall with an audible click when they contact the bridges. Refit the dampers and refill with oil (see **Chapter 5**).

5 Now turn down each adjusting nut two complete turns. This is turning it clockwise as seen from above. Move the spanner one flat at a time and count up to 12 flats.

6 Restart the engine and let it warm up. Adjust the throttle adjusting screws equally to give a fairly fast idling speed. Equal adjustment is checked by listening to the intensity of the hiss at each carburetter intake. Take a couple of feet of rubber or plastic tubing about $\frac{1}{4}$ inch in bore. Hold one end close to the ear and hold the free end adjacent to a carburetter intake (see **FIG 4:19**). Note the intensity of the hiss and move the tube to exactly the same position in the second intake. Adjust the throttle screws until the hiss is the same in both intakes. This will synchronize the throttles. Now check the mixture strength as follows:

Checking the mixture strength:

1 Follow the single-carburetter instructions from operation 4 in **Section 4:4**. If the engine speeds up, adjust each throttle screw by an equal amount.

2 Check the mixture strength as instructed in the same Section, starting with the lefthand carburetter. When this is correctly adjusted, turn to the righthand one. After adjusting this, return to the lefthand carburetter and recheck, because the carburetters are interdependent. The exhaust note should now be regular and even. If it is irregular, with some misfiring and a colourless exhaust, the mixture is too weak. If there is black exhaust smoke and a regular misfire the mixture is too rich (see **FIG 4:20**).

3 When adjustments are completed, refit the air cleaner. Due to the slight extra resistance to incoming air it is possible that the mixture may now be slightly rich. This is readily cured by turning the adjusting nut upwards or anticlockwise by two or three flats. If any adjustment to idling speed is necessary, each throttle screw must be turned an equal amount. The linkage must now be adjusted.

Linkage adjustment on engines with 8.8:1 compression ratio:

Check with **Facts and Figures** to determine the compression ratio of the engine fitted to your car. Then proceed as follows:

1 In **FIG 4:21** it will be seen that the throttle lever ends or pins work in forks in the levers attached to the throttle shafts. **There must be clearance between the pins and the lower arms of the forks when the throttles are closed.** Adjust as follows:

2 Slacken the throttle lever clamping bolts. Take a feeler gauge 70 thousandths of an inch thick, or a pack of feelers to make up that thickness. Insert the gauge between the throttle operating lever and the rod that interconnects the choke controls (see inset in **FIG 4:21**).

3 Press each throttle lever down until its pin rests lightly on the lower arm of the fork. Tighten the lever clamp bolts and remove the gauge. There should now be clearance between the pins and the forks.

Linkage adjustment on engines with 9.75:1 compression ratio:

Check in **Facts and Figures** to find whether this is the correct compression ratio of your engine. Then proceed as follows:

1 Remove the air cleaner assembly. Refer to **FIG 4:22**. Slacken the throttle lever clamp bolts and insert a feeler gauge six thousandths of an inch thick under each pin in turn. The pins will then be clear of the lower arms of the forks as shown in the inset top right in the illustration.

2 Tighten the lever clamp bolts. Connect the choke cable and check that the jet heads are right up to the adjusting nuts when the choke control knob is pushed fully in (see **FIG 4:6**).

3 Refit the air cleaners and check the fast-idling speed as follows:

Setting the fast-idling speed:

These instructions apply to all types of twin-carburetter installations.

1 Reconnect the choke cable in its original position. The clamp usually makes a small kink that will enable the correct position to be judged (see **FIG 4:17**).

2 The first half an inch of choke control movement will open the throttles without moving the jets. Pull the knob out approximately that distance and check that the jets have not been moved (see **FIG 4:23**).

3 Adjust the fast-idle screws to give an engine speed in the region of 1050 rev/min when hot (see **FIG 4:2** for location of screws).

Servicing the air cleaners:

Instructions for this operation are given in **Chapter 6**.

4:8 The fuel pump

An SU electric fuel pump is fitted. This pumps petrol from the rear-mounted tank. On early cars it is under the car on the lefthand side at the rear. Later cars have the pump fitted on the righthand side, under the floor of the luggage compartment (see **FIG 4:25**).

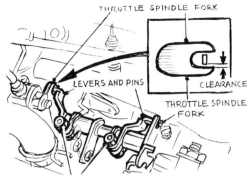

THROTTLE SPINDLE FORK
LEVERS AND PINS
CLEARANCE
THROTTLE SPINDLE FORK
THROTTLE SHAFT LEVER CLAMPING BOLTS

FIG 4:22 On engines with a 9.75 to 1 compression ratio and twin carburetters, set throttle lever pin and fork clearance as shown (see inset, top right)

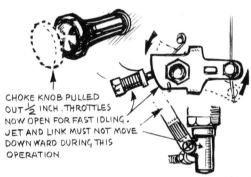

CHOKE KNOB PULLED OUT ½ INCH. THROTTLES NOW OPEN FOR FAST IDLING. JET AND LINK MUST NOT MOVE DOWNWARD DURING THIS OPERATION

FIG 4:23 Initial movement of choke (mixture) control knob opens the throttle for fast idling. In this position the jets must not move downwards to enrich the mixture

BEWARE OF FIRE!

FIG 4:24 Checking that petrol is being pumped to the carburetter. The righthand view shows how hose clips are released with pliers

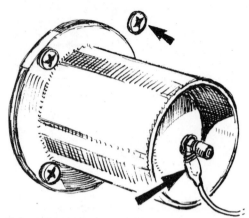

FIG 4:25 Electrical connections to the petrol pump must be clean and tight. The earth connection goes to the screw at the top. This illustration shows the later type of installation

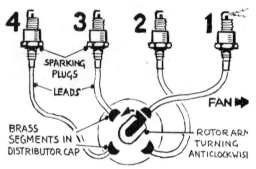

FIG 4:26 How the distributor rotor arm turns to distribute spark current to the plugs in the correct firing order of 1, 3, 4 and 2

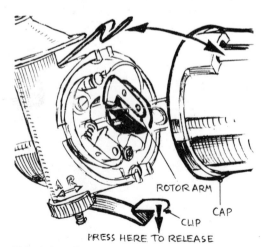

FIG 4:27 Remove the distributor cap by releasing the two spring clips. The rotor arm is a push fit

Because the pump is below the level of petrol in the tank, disconnecting the feed pipe hose means draining the tank, or plugging the hose as it is withdrawn from the pump. As we think it inadvisable for our readers to be involved in operations that may lead to floods of petrol, we have decided not to give instructions on servicing the fuel pump.

If trouble with the electric pump is suspected:

There are some useful checks to be made on the pump. The first is to listen to the clicks that the pump makes when it is working. If the ignition switch is turned on after the car has been standing all night, the pump will make a series of fairly rapid clicks, then slow right down. If the engine is started and allowed to idle the pump will be heard to make an occasional click. In this case the pump would seem to be in good order.

If fuel starvation is suspected because the engine will not start, or if it stops without apparent reason (see **Solve-it-yourself**), do the following:

1 With ignition switched off, disconnect the fuel pipe from the carburetter float chamber (see **Section 4:5**).

2 Hold the open end down inside a suitable container (see **FIG 4:24**). **Take all sensible precautions against fire.**

3 Get a second person to switch on the ignition. Petrol should gush from the hose in regular spurts. Switch off and reconnect the hose.

If the spurts continue strongly, the pump is probably working well. If they die down fairly rapidly there may be an obstruction in the pipes. If there is no delivery, keep the ignition switched on and try a light tap on the body of the pump (not the plastic end cap which carries the terminal connection). The pump may then start to click. If it does not, check the electrical connections, including the earth wire to the body (see **FIG 4:25**).

If the pump clicks rapidly at first and continues to click at a fair speed even though the engine is not running, suspect an air leak on the suction side of the pump. Check all hose connections. An air leak may also give rise to a petrol leak. If the pump struggles to operate in all conditions, there may be an obstruction in the pipe to the carburetter.

Any problems with a pump that has seen long service are best cured by an exchange with a new or reconditioned one. Those who feel competent to repair and adjust a faulty pump will find full instructions in the Autobook 1100/1300 Workshop Manual (see the last page of Chapter 7 in this book).

THE IGNITION SYSTEM

4:9 How the system works

Engine power is derived from the ignition of a compressed mixture of air and petrol. The production of the necessary sparks for ignition is the task of the battery, the coil, the distributor and the sparking plugs. These sparks must be healthy and must occur at precise moments in the cycle of engine operations. It is the function of the distributor to induce the coil to produce current for sparks, by opening and closing a pair of contacts. It must also distribute this current to the sparking plugs at the right time and in the correct firing order (see **FIG 4:26**). This is done by a rotor arm and four adjacent segments in the distributor cap, leading to wires connected to the sparking plugs.

Adjustments are needed to compensate for wear of the contact points and sparking plug electrodes. Although not normally essential, adjustment of the ignition timing may be needed with a secondhand car or to set it for a particular grade of petrol.

Location of distributor:

The distributor is mounted in front of the engine as shown in **FIG 3:19**. It will be recognized by the five thick wires leading from the cover to the coil and sparking plugs. Early cars have a protective sheath over the cap to protect it from damp. Later cars have a baffle fitted inside the grille.

Removing the cap and the rotor arm:

1 To remove the cap ease off the two spring clips (see **FIG 4:27**). On early cars it will be necessary to peel back the protective sheath. The rotor arm is a push fit, but if it is tight, lever it upwards very gently with a screwdriver.

Adjusting the contact breaker points:

2 **FIG 4:28** shows the distributor platform. To check the gap between the points the engine must be turned until the points are opened to their fullest extent (see inset, top right).

3 To turn the engine, remove the sparking plugs, engage top gear and push the car forward (not back). On cars with automatic transmission there is an aperture above the dipstick and this is covered by a rubber grommet (see **FIG 4:29**). With the grommet removed, the engine may be turned by levering on the starter teeth with a screwdriver.

There is a device available from most accessory shops that eliminates the need for turning the engine. This slips over the distributor cams and the gap can then be checked with the cams in any position.

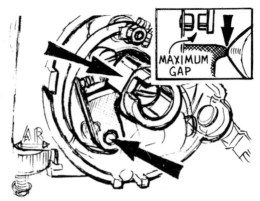

FIG 4:28 Removal of the distributor cap and rotor arm reveals the contact breaker platform. The top arrow points to the cams and the lower arrow to the pivot for the moving contact

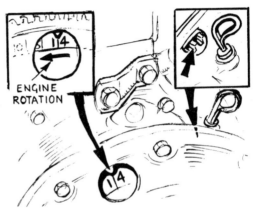

FIG 4:29 For ignition timing on cars with automatic transmission, turn the engine by levering on the gear teeth with a screwdriver (top right). The flywheel marks are shown top left. Rubber grommets cover both apertures

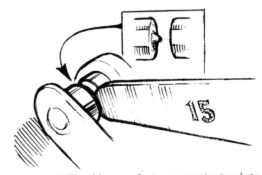

FIG 4:30 Checking gap between contact points by inserting a fifteen thousandths of an inch feeler gauge. Inset shows how a pip on one point makes accurate checking impossible

FIG 4:31 To adjust the contact points, slacken the screw on the left and turn a screwdriver in the notches shown on the right.

FIG 4:32 The connection between piston position and flywheel markings when a spark occurs before top dead centre (BTDC)

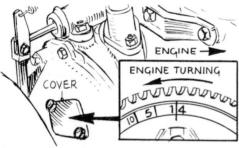

FIG 4:33 On cars with manual gearchange, remove the cover from the clutch housing to check the timing marks on the flywheel (see inset)

FIG 4:34 No. 1 sparking plug is at the end of the engine nearest to the fan

4 Having set the engine so that the points are the maximum distance apart, insert a fifteen thousandth of an inch feeler gauge between them (see **FIG 4:30**). **Make sure the feeler blade is clean and free from oil.** The gauge should be a sliding fit without actually opening the points still more. There is some permissible latitude. If the gap is not less than .014 inch or more than .016 inch there is no need to alter the setting.

5 To adjust the points, refer to **FIG 4:31** and barely slacken the securing screw. Insert a screwdriver blade as shown. The blade should be wide enough to engage in the grooves. Turn the blade clockwise to reduce the gap and anticlockwise to increase it. Tighten the securing screw and recheck the gap.

6 It is always advisable, after adjusting the points gap, to check the ignition timing, as large alterations in the points gap may upset the timing by several degrees. Refer to **Section 4:10** to carry out this operation.

7 Refit the rotor arm, locating the moulded key over the drive slot in the spindle. Push the rotor arm fully home.

8 The moulded cap has locating slots in its lower face. Make sure the cap is seated correctly and secure it with the spring clips. Replace the protective sheath and the sparking plugs.

Condition of the contact points:

If when checking the gap you notice that the points are blackened and the faces are uneven, do not attempt to adjust them. There is often some slight sparking at the points and this causes a build-up or pip to form on one point, with a corresponding depression in the other (see **FIG 4:30**). This makes it impossible to check the gap accurately and the best cure is to fit a new set of points. This is not an expensive operation.

If you feel confident about renewing them, buy a new contact set, preferably of the latest one-piece type. Remove nut at top of **FIG 4:28** and the screw just visible behind the top lefthand arrow. Fit the new set, taking care to assemble the electrical connections correctly under the top nut. Set the contact gap and use the lubricant provided. One drop is enough for the pivot (lowest arrow). If the earlier type of assembly is being fitted, ensure that the insulating bush is fitted in the spring eye, just under the connections.

4:10 Ignition timing

There are two methods of checking the accuracy of the ignition timing and these are called 'Static' and 'Stroboscopic'. Static timing is the method used when the engine is stationary. Stroboscopic timing is a very accurate method that requires some skill and a special 'strobe' lamp. This is used to check the timing while the engine is running (see **FIG 4:38**).

Static timing:

1 To check the ignition timing by this method the engine must be positioned with No. 1 piston at the top of the cylinder on the compression stroke. This is known as **Top Dead Centre** and it is always identified by the initials **TDC**. Markings are stamped on the flywheel to enable this position to be set. **FIGS 4:32** and **4:33** show the numbers 1 and 4 separately by a vertical line. This line is the TDC mark for pistons 1 and 4. Piston 1 is at the fan end of the engine (see **FIG 4:34**), and so too is No. 1 sparking plug. **FIG 4:33** shows how the markings are exposed by removing a small cover on top of the clutch housing. See **FIG 4:29** if automatic transmission is fitted.

2 Remove this cover. Take out the sparking plugs so that the engine can be turned easily to bring the TDC mark into view. Get someone to push the car slowly forward in top gear whilst you look into a mirror to see the reflected image of the marks. TDC is indicated when the vertical line on the flywheel is in line with the small pointer on the flywheel housing. If the car has automatic transmission, turn the engine by following the instructions given in **Section 4:9**, operation 3. In every case, set the timing after turning the engine forward, **never after turning it backwards.**

3 To make sure that No. 1 piston is on the compression stroke, take off the distributor cap and look at the position of the rotor arm. The short brass segment on the rotor arm should be facing No. 1 segment in the distributor cap (see **FIG 4:26**). Another check is to put a thumb over No. 1 sparking plug hole as the engine is turned. As No. 1 piston rises on its compression stroke, pressure will tend to blow the thumb away from the hole. The reason for all this checking is that pistons 1 and 4 rise together, but it is only No. 1 piston that is on the compression stroke and will be ready for ignition.

4 Note that ignition actually occurs a few degrees **before top dead centre (BTDC)**. The position varies according to model and all the variations are listed in **Facts and Figures** in **Chapter 8**.

5 Having determined the correct timing for your car, remove the distributor vacuum pipe and set the flywheel markings correctly. In advance of the 1/4 mark for TDC there are three indicator lines stamped with the figures 5, 10 and sometimes 15. These are positions in degrees in advance of TDC. It will be necessary to estimate the position if, for

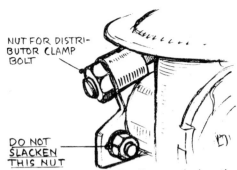

FIG 4:35 To turn the distributor, slacken the clamping nut. Do not confuse with the lower nuts

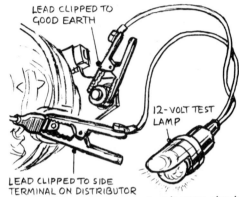

FIG 4:36 How to connect a test lamp to check the moment when the contact points open

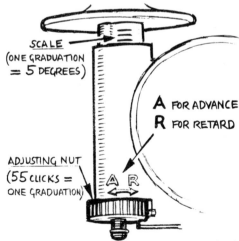

FIG 4:37 The micrometer nut on the distributor is used to make fine adjustments to the ignition timing

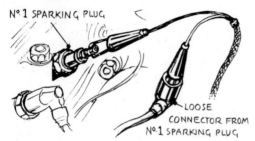

FIG 4:38 How to connect a stroboscopic timing lamp to No. 1 sparking plug and the plug connector

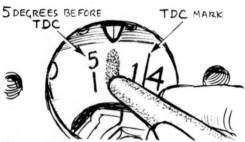

FIG 4:39 To use a stroboscopic timing lamp, make a chalk mark on the flywheel at the correct position for ignition timing. The mark is shown at 3 degrees before top dead centre by approximation

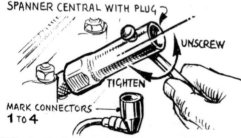

FIG 4:40 Removing a sparking plug. Do not let the spanner tilt to one side or the plug insulator may be fractured

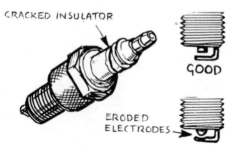

FIG 4:41 When inspecting sparking plugs, look for a cracked insulator and heavily eroded electrodes

example, it happens to be 3 deg. BTDC. Turn the engine until the correct position is in line with the pointer on the housing (see **FIGS 4:32** and **4:39**).

6 Remove the rotor arm from the distributor and check the position of the contact breaker points. They should be just on the point of opening. To adjust, slacken the clamp bolt at the base of the distributor (see **FIG 4:35**). Turn the distributor body clockwise to advance the opening of the points and in an anticlockwise direction to retard the opening. Whilst you are doing this, try to turn the cams in a clockwise direction. This will take up the slack in the drive. Turn the distributor to the position where the points are just about to open. Hold this position whilst you tighten the clamp bolt. **Do not overtighten.**

7 A more accurate way of timing is to connect a 12-volt test lamp between the low-tension terminal on the distributor body and a good earth, as shown in **FIG 4:36**. Switch on the ignition. Slacken the clamp bolt on the distributor moderately (see **FIG 4:35**) and turn the distributor body in an anticlockwise direction so that the points are fully closed. Now turn it slowly in a clockwise direction. When the lamp glows the points are just opening. Tighten the clamp bolt, disconnect the lamp and switch off the ignition.

8 Complete operations 7 and 8 in **Section 4:9**, replace the cover on top of the flywheel housing and reconnect the vacuum pipe.

9 Final adjustments to the timing can be made by turning the micro-adjuster on the distributor body (see **FIG 4:37**). By turning the knurled nut clockwise the ignition will be retarded. Turning it anticlockwise will advance the ignition. The direction for turning is indicated by the letters A for advance and R for retard, with appropriate arrows. Each graduation on the scale is equal to 5 deg. on the flywheel or 55 clicks on the ratchet of the knurled nut. These very fine adjustments are usually made on a trial and error basis to obtain the best performance from different grades of petrol. Generally speaking, low grades of petrol call for a retarded ignition point. This is one that occurs nearer to TDC than the standard setting.

Stroboscopic timing:

1 This method of timing must be done with the engine running at idling speed, but not more than 600 rev/min. If a tachometer (revolution indicator) is fitted an accurate idling speed can be set by adjusting the throttle screw(s) (see **Section 4:4**). Without a tachometer it is impossible to gauge the idling speed, but if the engine is running at idle it should be satisfactory.

2 Stroboscopic timing lamps can be obtained from most motor accessory shops. The lamp is used as follows:

Disconnect the lead from No. 1 plug (nearest the fan) and connect one lead from the lamp to the plug and the other lead from the lamp to the metal contact up inside the loose connector (see **FIG 4:38**). Refer to **FIGS 4:29** and **4:33** and take off the cover on top of the flywheel housing. Uncouple the vacuum advance pipe from the distributor at the union nut below the plug lead in **FIG 7:33**.

3 Follow the instructions given in operation 5 under 'Static Timing'. Mark the appropriate timing mark with a chalk line (see **FIG 4:39**).

4 Start the engine and let it idle. The lamp will begin to flash on and off. This has the effect of making the timing mark look as if it is stationary and its exact position can be seen in relation to the pointer. If the light shows the timing mark to be to the right of the pointer, the timing is too advanced and if it is in front of or to the left of the pointer it is too far retarded.

5 Slacken the clamp bolt of the distributor (see **FIG 4:35**). Turn the distributor in a clockwise direction to advance the timing and anticlockwise to retard it. If it is only slightly out, use the micro-adjuster. Watch the mark and align it with the pointer.

6 Tighten the clamp bolt and reconnect the vacuum advance pipe. Replace the cover, disconnect the lamp and reconnect the lead to No. 1 plug. Adjust the engine to the correct idling speed (see **Section 4:4**).

4:11 Sparking plug condition

The sparking plugs should be removed regularly for cleaning and inspection, say at every 3000 miles. The condition of the electrodes will often give valuable information on fuel mixture strength and ignition timing.

Before removing them, mark the plug lead connectors 1, 2, 3 and 4, starting with No. 1 at the fan end of the engine (see **FIG 4:34**). It will then be possible to refit them correctly. Remove the plugs as shown in **FIG 4:40**, blowing dirt from around the seatings when the plugs are half-unscrewed. Take care that the box spanner does not tilt and fracture the plug insulator (see **FIG 4:41**).

The normal deposit on the electrodes should be light brown or a greyish tan in colour (see **FIG 4:42**). A white or yellowish deposit is also to be expected in an engine that has been used for long spells of steady driving or town work. Wet deposits of black sludge indicate oil fouling due to a badly worn engine. This deposit should not be confused with petrol wetting caused by excessive use of the choke when trying to start a reluctant engine.

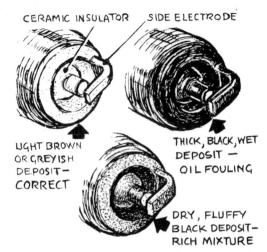

FIG 4:42 The type of deposit on a sparking plug is a useful indication of engine operating conditions

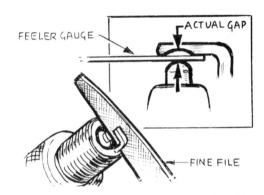

FIG 4:43 Use a fine file to clean-up sparking plug electrodes. Accurate measurements of electrode gap are impossible if the points are badly eroded (see inset)

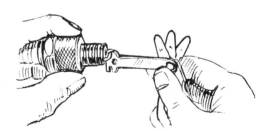

FIG 4:44 Never adjust sparking plug gap by bending centre electrode. The typical gauge and setting tool is handy for gap measurement and for bending the side electrode

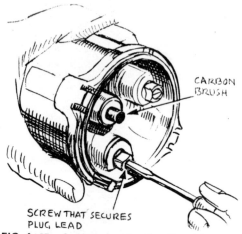

FIG 4:45 A view inside the distributor cap showing the screws that secure the plug leads. The carbon brush in the centre must project and move freely

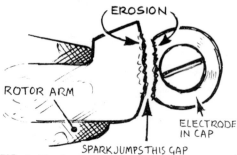

FIG 4:46 Sparks jump the gap between the rotor arm and the segment in the distributor cap. Slight erosion of the brass parts is normal

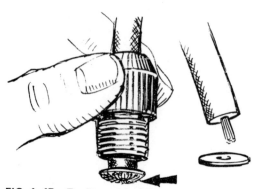

FIG 4:47 To fit a new cable to the centre of the coil, bare the copper wires and spread them fanwise over the washer. The coil is shown in FIG 3:19

Dry, black fluffy deposits are usually caused by incomplete combustion. This may be due to an excessively rich mixture, to over-choking, long periods of idling or to defective ignition.

Overheated sparking plugs have a white or blistered appearance of the electrodes and the side electrode may be badly eroded. The cause of this may be ineffective cooling, weak mixture, incorrect ignition timing or long spells of high speed running. Attention to engine tuning may be necessary to cure this trouble. Normally the plugs should be of the type recommended in **Facts and Figures**.

4:12 Cleaning and adjusting sparking plugs

Sand blasting the electrodes to clean them is recommended practice, but as this must be done at a service station, it may not be convenient. If not heavily fouled, a light wire brushing over the electrodes and the threads is all that will be required. **Do not wire brush the ceramic insulator** (see **FIG 4:42**). The metal scratches left by the wire brush may shortcircuit the spark.

Soak the fouled plugs in neat vinegar for about 24 hours. This will soften the carbon deposits. Any stubborn carbon can be scraped off with a matchstick or a sliver of wood.

After cleaning the plugs, check the electrodes.

Usually the end of the centre electrode is rounded off and there is a matching depression in the side electrode (see **FIG 4:43**). Clean up the electrodes with a small fine file as shown. To ensure getting a good spark keep the edges square. Filing the electrodes will also help to give a true gap. A false reading will be obtained if the electrodes are eroded, as can be seen in the inset.

To adjust the gap, bend the side electrode only. **Do not bend the centre electrode.** If the gap is too wide, tap the side electrode lightly to bring it nearer the central one. If it is too close, lever the side electrode away with a small screwdriver. Special gap setting tools can be obtained from accessory shops. These have combined feeler gauges and a tool for bending the electrodes (see **FIG 4:44**). The correct gap is 24 to 26 thousandths of an inch (.024 to .026).

Clean the gasket seatings before refitting the plugs and check the gaskets. Renew them if they are severely flattened to less than half their original thickness.

After approximately 10,000 miles the plugs should be renewed. As they are relatively cheap, it is wise to fit new plugs in order to keep engine performance at its peak.

4:13 Servicing distributor, cap and plug leads
The cap:

Check the distributor cap when you are checking the points. Wipe it clean, and examine all surfaces for cracks. Look for a faint black line between the brass electrodes. This is known as 'tracking' and is caused by surface current leakage. The only cure is to renew the cap. Ensure that the small carbon brush in the centre of the cap is sound and is free to move under pressure from the spring (see **FIG 4:45**). It should protrude about $\frac{1}{8}$ inch and spring out when released after it has been pressed in. Scrape the brass electrodes inside the cap with a sharp knife to remove deposits and wipe the cap clean. **The rotor arm does not make actual contact with these electrodes** (see **FIG 4:46**).

Clean the brass segment on the rotor arm with petrol. Do not file the end or rub it with emerycloth. The erosion is normal and is due to sparking (see **FIG 4:46**).

The plug leads:

Examine the high-tension leads to the plugs by doubling the cable and checking for cracks. Running the engine in the dark helps to detect insulation failure. Bluish electrical discharges will be seen where any leaks occur (see **FIG 7:33**).

Before removing them, mark the connectors 1 to 4, starting at the fan end (see **FIG 4:34**). Renew cables one at a time to avoid confusing the connectors.

The cables are secured by a pointed screw that penetrates the insulation, so there is no need to bare the wire. Remove the screw and pull out the old cable (see **FIG 4:45**).

Smear the end of the new cable with silicone grease, push it fully home into the cap and refit the screw. At the sparking plug end pull the insulating cover off the cable and peel off the protective sheath. Remove the metal clip and refit it to the new cable, fit the protective sheath and insert the clip and cable into the cover. Some covers may be found to be screwed onto the cable. Remove these by unscrewing. Refit by screwing into the wire core of the cable. The correct sequence of connections to the sparking plugs is shown in **FIG 4:26**.

The high-tension lead from the distributor to the coil is fitted at the coil end through a knurled nut. Bare about $\frac{1}{4}$ of an inch of the wires of the new cable, and thread it through the nut. Fit the brass washer and fan out the wires as shown in **FIG 4:47**. Later models may be fitted with a modified push-fit type. The location of the coil is shown in **FIG 3:19**.

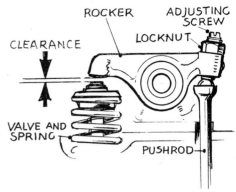

FIG 4:48 The arrows indicate the clearance between the tip of the rocker and the valve stem. The correct gap is 12 thousandths of an inch when the valve is closed and the engine is cold

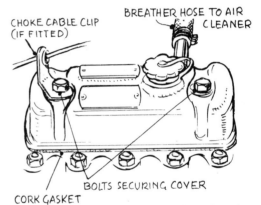

FIG 4:49 Rocker cover details, showing securing bolts

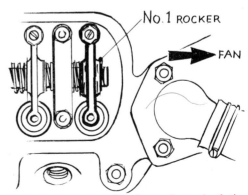

FIG 4:50 No. 1 rocker is at the end of the engine nearest to the fan

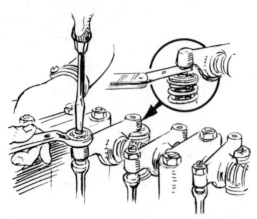

FIG 4:51 Method of checking and adjusting valve clearance. Inset shows feeler gauge in position

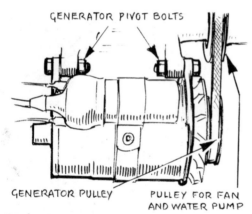

GENERATOR PIVOT BOLTS

GENERATOR PULLEY

PULLEY FOR FAN AND WATER PUMP

FIG 4:52 A view looking down on the generator to show the top pivot bolts and the pulleys

FIG 4:53 Check the belt tension midway between the top pulleys. Total movement between arrows should be about $\frac{1}{2}$ inch

THE ENGINE

4:14 Adjusting the clearances in the valve rocker gear

The cover over the valves and rockers is shown in **FIG 4:49**. When this is removed you will see the valves and their rockers as shown in **FIG 4:51**. There are eight valves, four of them being inlet valves to control the entry of petrol and air mixture into the four cylinders. The remaining four are exhaust valves to allow the burnt gases to leave the cylinders. When the engine is turned you will see how pushrods and rockers operate the valves in an orderly sequence. Without being too technical, we must explain that certain clearances are essential in the valve-operating mechanism and these may increase due to wear. The clearance is taken up when each valve is open, so that it can only be measured between a rocker tip and the end of the valve stem **when the valve is closed** (see **FIG 4:48**). **This must be done when the engine is cold, the correct clearance being 12 thousandths of an inch** (.012).

The clearances may increase slightly in the engine of a new car, and it is a good plan to check them after about 6000 miles. After buying a secondhand car it is wise to check them fairly soon, particularly if there is a light mechanical clatter coming from the region of the rocker cover. Setting the correct clearances will help to quieten a noisy engine.

Carrying out the operation:

Before lifting the rocker cover, buy a new cover gasket, as it is often damaged during removal (see **FIG 4:49**).

1 If there is a rubber hose between the rocker cover and the air cleaner, pull this off the cover.
2 Remove the bolts securing the cover. One bolt secures the choke cable clip on some models.
3 Lift the cover, tapping it lightly with a piece of wood if it sticks. This is where the cork gasket may be broken.

The engine must now be turned and this operation has already been described under 'Adjusting the contact breaker points' in **Section 4:9**.

It is not advisable to apply pressure to the fan belt and then to pull the engine round by means of the fan. **The fan blades are plastic and may be broken.**

While the engine is turning, watch the valves. You will see that they open and close in a certain sequence. A valve is fully open when it is fully depressed. Note that the rocker has no clearance at this stage. Let the valve rise and turn the engine a fraction after the valve has stopped rising. You will now find that there is clearance between the rocker tip and the end of the valve stem (see **FIG 4:48**). To determine the position where the clearance must be measured, work to the following plan:

Check No. 1 rocker with No. 8 valve fully open.
Check No. 3 rocker with No. 6 valve fully open.
Check No. 5 rocker with No. 4 valve fully open.
Check No. 2 rocker with No. 7 valve fully open.
Check No. 8 rocker with No. 1 valve fully open.
Check No. 6 rocker with No. 3 valve fully open.
Check No. 4 rocker with No. 5 valve fully open.
Check No. 7 rocker with No. 2 valve fully open.

The numbers on each line add up to nine and this fact may be used to avoid frequent reference to the table. No. 1 rocker is nearest the fan (see **FIG 4 : 50**).

The actual checking and adjusting :
When you are satisfied that one particular valve is closed and its opposite number is fully open according to the table, check the clearance with feeler gauges as shown in **FIG 4 : 51**.

If it exceeds 12 thousandths of an inch, adjust as follows:

1 Slacken the locknut until the screw is just capable of being turned with a screwdriver. Turn clockwise to reduce the gap. If the clearance is less than the stipulated figure, turn the screw anticlockwise. Hold the nut while turning the screw.

2 When there is just a slight nip on the feeler, remove it. Hold the screw stationary and tighten the locknut. Check the clearance again in case the screw has moved.

3 After all clearances have been checked, prepare the cover for refitting.

4 Remove all traces of the old cork gasket from the cover and engine faces. Make sure no dirt remains in the head. Fit the new gasket and replace the cover. **Do not overtighten the bolts or the cover will be distorted.** Refit the breather hose and sparking plugs, start the engine and check for oil leaks.

4 : 15 The fan belt
The belt links three pulleys, and is driven by the one on the engine crankshaft. The front one at the top drives the electrical generator and the rear one the fan and water pump (see **FIG 4 : 52**).

After a long spell of use the belt will stretch and may slip, there may be oil on the pulleys, and the belt may even begin to disintegrate. If you have bought a secondhand car, examine the belt at once. If it looks cracked and frayed it is best renewed (see **FIG 7 : 31**).

A belt is most likely to break when you are driving, and then the red ignition warning light will glow and will not go out at any engine speed. This is the reason why we recommend you to carry a spare belt in your tool kit, because it **is** possible to fit a belt by the roadside. If you are not prepared to do this, proceed **slowly** to a service station. This will avoid overheating due to the lack of fan and water pump cooling. Remember too, that you will not be charging the battery.

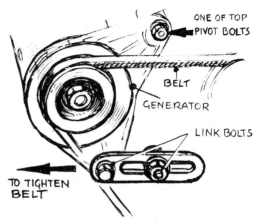

FIG 4 : 54 With pivot and link bolts slack, tighten belt by moving generator in direction of arrow. Moving in the opposite direction will slacken the belt

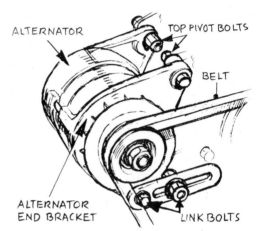

FIG 4 : 55 If an alternator is fitted instead of a generator (see FIG 7 : 56), do not lift the alternator by the body but only by the end bracket

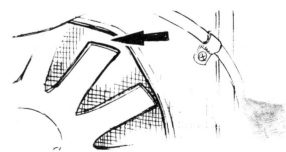

FIG 4 : 56 Clearance in the radiator cowling will enable the belt to be removed or fitted over the fan blades

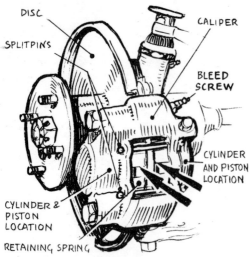

FIG 4:57 The fixed-caliper front brake fitted to earlier 1100 models. The arrows point to the friction pads. Note that there are two cylinders and pistons

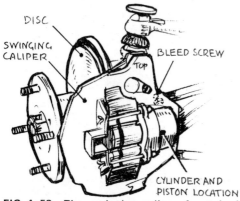

FIG 4:58 The swinging-caliper front brake fitted to later Mk 2 and all 1300 models. Note that there is only one cylinder

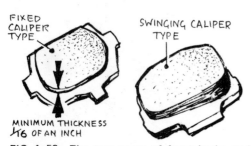

FIG 4:59 The two types of front brake pad. Renewal of the later type shown on the right is best left to a service station

Adjusting the belt:

A belt must not be too tight or it will overload the generator and water pump bearings. If it slips, your battery may be under-charged and you may suffer from overheating. The tension is checked by lifting and pressing on the belt as shown in **FIG 4:53**. The position selected must be midway between the top pulleys. If the total movement is about $\frac{1}{2}$ inch the tension is correct. If you feel that adjustment is needed proceed as follows:

When a generator is fitted:

This is the type shown in **FIGS 4:52** and **4:54**.
1 Slacken off the two pivot bolts on the upper brackets. Under the pulley is a slotted link that is secured by two bolts (see **FIG 4:54**). Slacken these bolts and lift the generator with one hand so that it swings outwards to tighten the belt. Push the generator down to slacken the belt. Having found the right position, tighten the slotted link bolts first. Check the tension again after tightening the remaining bolts.

When an alternator is fitted:

This is the type shown in **FIG 4:55**. Slacken the four bolts (arrowed). **Do not lift on the alternator body to adjust the belt.** Apply pressure to the end bracket as indicated in the illustration. Tighten the bolts and recheck the tension.

Renewing the fan belt:

Never try to lever the belt over the pulleys or the flanges may be damaged.
1 Slacken the securing bolts of the generator or alternator. Push the generator fully down or apply pressure on the alternator end bracket to remove all tension on the belt.
2 Lift the belt off the generator/alternator pulley, then off the crankshaft (lower) pulley. Very carefully manoeuvre the belt over the fan blades towards the radiator. The radiator cowling has a recess at the top righthand corner to admit the fan belt (see **FIG 4:56**).
3 Fit the new belt through the cowling recess and carefully over the fan blades. Wind it round the lower pulley and then over the generator/alternator and fan pulleys. Adjust the tension as previously described.

THE BRAKING SYSTEM

4:16 Servicing the brakes

There are disc brakes on the front and drum brakes on the rear. The discs and drums rotate with the wheels and braking is achieved by the pressure of friction-lined pads or shoes against the discs or drums. This pressure is transmitted from the brake pedal to the brakes by hydraulic fluid carried in pipes.

The handbrake is mechanically operated and works on the rear wheels only. There is no independent adjustment for it, but excessive travel of the lever is taken up after adjustment at the rear wheels (see **Section 4:17**).

Wear on the front disc pads is taken up automatically and there is no adjustment. Two types of caliper are used, the fixed type and the swinging type. The fixed type caliper is fitted to all Mk 1 models and some early Mk 2 with synchromesh transmission (see **FIG 4:57**). The swinging caliper replaced the fixed one on later Mk 2 models and all the 1300 range (see **FIG 4:58**). All Mk 2 automatic transmission models are fitted with the swinging type. For technical reasons we are confining the following instructions to fixed caliper brakes only.

If your car is a new one it will not be necessary to look at the front brake pads for some considerable time. If it is a secondhand one with a high mileage it would be advisable to check the pads, particularly before attempting a long journey. **When renewing pads it is absolutely essential to ensure that the correct type is obtained. Never mix different types of braking material. It is also advisable to renew the pads of both front brakes at the same time.**

Inspecting and renewing brake pads:

Fixed caliper type:

Jack up the car and remove the road wheel as described in **Chapter 2, Section 2:2** and in **Section 4:24**.

It is possible to check the thickness of the friction lining by looking through the gaps in the retaining spring, as shown in **FIG 4:57**. The friction material is immediately adjacent to the disc and if it is down to $\frac{1}{16}$ inch in thickness, the pads must be renewed. Even when there is $\frac{1}{8}$ inch of material still available it is wise to consider fitting new pads, especially before a motoring holiday. If renewal is indicated do the following:

1 Refer to **FIG 4:57**. Scrape off dirt from around the two splitpins and straighten the legs of each one, using a hammer and punch to bring them together (see **FIG 4:60**). Grip the underside of the head with a pair of pliers and tap on the pliers to extract the pins. **The splitpins must be scrapped and replaced by new ones.** Remove the pad retaining spring.

2 Grip the backplate of one pad with thin-nosed pliers and at the same time partially rotate it to ease it out. As the pad is pulled out a thin anti-squeak shim that is between the backplate and piston may come out with it (see **FIG 4:61**). Save this shim so that it can be replaced in the original position. Leave the second pad where it is for the moment.

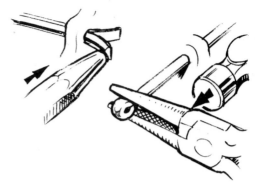

FIG 4:60 To remove the pad-retaining split-pins, tap the ends together with a hammer and punch (left). With thin-nosed pliers gripping the underside of the splitpin eye, tapping on the pliers will remove the pin

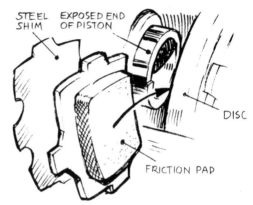

FIG 4:61 Front brake pad and shim removed to show the exposed end of the piston

FIG 4:62 Using a strip of wood to press a brake piston back into its cylinder

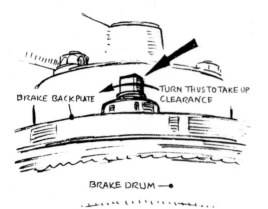

FIG 4:63 With the road wheel removed it is possible to see the rear brake adjuster

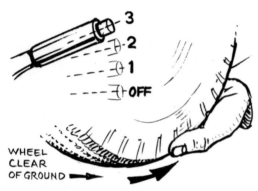

FIG 4:64 To check rear brakes apply hand-brake three notches. Both rear wheels must take the same heavy pull to move them

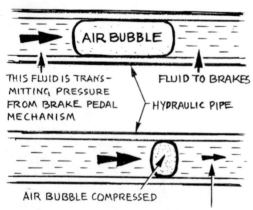

FIG 4:65 Because air is compressible, bubbles of it in the hydraulic system may give a 'spongy' feeling to brake pedal application

3 Looking into the empty recess you will now see the piston that pushes the pad on to the disc. Look for any signs of hydraulic fluid leakage past the piston. It can be detected by examining the dirt around the piston and in the recess. Wet deposits will be darker than dry dust. Brake fluid has a distinctive smell. Check it by smelling the fluid in your spare can.

An abnormally low level in the master cylinder reservoir calls for immediate consultation with your garage (see **Section 6:10** in **Chapter 6**).

Scrape out the dirt. Clean the exposed sides of the piston and the recess with methylated spirits. **Do not use petrol or other solvents.** It is not possible to get behind the piston with your fingers, but if you thread a strip of cloth around it by poking it with a piece of wire, the cloth can be pulled to and fro. Make sure the brake disc is clean and dry. It may look scored on the braking surfaces but this is normally nothing to worry about unless excessive wear is apparent (see **FIG 7:52**). If in doubt, consult your service station.

4 The piston should now be pushed back into its bore. This is to provide extra clearance for new pads or when changing the positions of the original pads. If the pads are worn unevenly but are not less than $\frac{1}{16}$ inch thick anywhere, they can be changed over in the caliper to equalise the wear. The piston may not need pushing back if the same pad is being refitted. Push the piston back with a flat lever (see **FIG 4:62**). Do not use force and do not lever against the disc. As the piston is pressed in, fluid will rise in the master cylinder reservoir. Check the level to make sure fluid will not overflow. If the level is well below the filler neck it should be all right. To be on the safe side, tie a long piece of rag around the filler neck to soak up any overflow, **but be careful when you are removing it as the fluid will damage paintwork.**

5 Fit the anti-squeak shim and pad into the recess, making sure the pad can move freely. If a new pad binds, file off the high spots on the edges of the metal backing plate. **Be extremely careful not to touch the friction material with dirty hands, and at all times keep oil and dirt from the pads, the discs and the pistons.** Push in the new splitpins part way to keep the pad in place and then attend to the second pad.

6 After completing the work on the pads, fit the pad retaining spring and the new splitpins. Open the legs of the splitpins moderately. Refit the wheels. Operate the brake pedal to take up. the clearance between the pads and the disc. Check the fluid level in the master cylinder and top it up if necessary (see **Chapter 5, Section 5:3, (5)**).

Swinging caliper type:

The operations are identical to those for removing the brake pads on the fixed caliper, except that there is only one piston to contend with and the brake pads are steeply angled (see **FIG 4:59**). This taper on the brake pads prohibits interchanging to even out wear. The pads must be replaced in the same positions or new ones fitted. It is also impossible to check the thickness without removing the retaining spring. As the caliper must be re-centralised after fitting new pads we advise the owners to entrust the whole operation to a service station.

4:17 Rear brake adjustment

Unlike the automatic adjustment on the front brakes, the rear brake shoes must be adjusted manually. Adjustment will be necessary when the travel of the brake pedal and the handbrake is abnormally long before braking is felt.

1 Jack up the rear wheels in turn (see **Chapter 2, Section 2:2**). As a safety precaution, chock the front wheels. Remove the road wheel. Release the handbrake.

2 Refer to **FIG 4:63** which shows the location of the square-headed adjuster behind the brake drum. Do not use a thin open-ended spanner to turn the adjuster if it is tight, or the corners may be rounded off. Use an adjustable spanner with thick jaws or one of the special square-holed spanners sold for the purpose. Do not force the adjuster if it is exceptionally tight. Try some penetrating oil on the threads and if this is no cure it will be necessary for a garage to rectify the fault.

3 Spin the rear wheel or brake drum and turn the adjuster nut clockwise (viewed from the back), You will feel the clicks as you turn. Continue to turn the wheel and the adjuster until the brake is firmly applied and you cannot turn either. You may find that the adjuster will lock the brake before it reaches another 'click' position. Do not force it, but return to the preceding 'click' position.

4 With the drum locked, turn the adjuster in an anticlockwise direction until the drum just turns freely. Repeat this operation on the other side.

5 Apply the handbrake or the footbrake two or three times and then check the adjustment again on both sides. While the wheels are off, use an oil can at the point indicated in **FIG 4:67**.

6 Finally, apply the handbrake three notches on the ratchet and check that the wheels require heavy and equal hand pressure to turn them (see **FIG 4:64**). If after adjustment, there is still excessive travel on the handbrake have the mechanism adjusted by a service station. This failure is most likely to be due to badly worn rear brake linings.

STAINS HERE ARE GENERALLY DUE TO LEAKAGE FROM ENGINE

FRONT OF CAR

STAINS DUE TO LEAKING BRAKE FLUID

FIG 4:66 Stains on the garage floor may help in tracing brake fluid leaks. Note location so that the stains are not confused with oil leaks from the engine

APPLY A FEW DROPS OF OIL TO THIS JOINT

FIG 4:67 The rear brake bleed screws are behind the brakes as shown

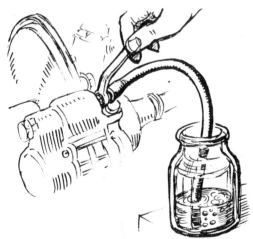

FIG 4:68 Bleeding a front brake. The bleed screw projects from the back of the caliper

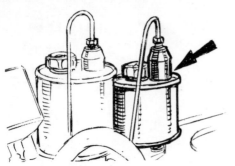

FIG 4:69 The clutch master cylinder and reservoir is the smaller of the two

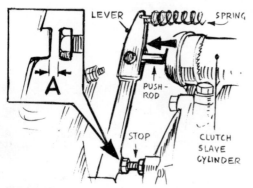

FIG 4:70 To adjust the clutch stop, pull lever in direction of arrow (top right). Inset on the left shows where gap must be measured (A)

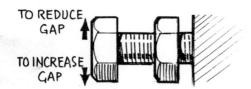

FIG 4:71 How to turn the clutch stop to alter the gap

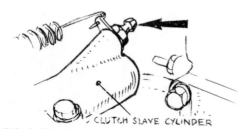

FIG 4:72 Location of the bleed screw on the clutch slave cylinder

4:18 Bleeding the braking system

This is not a normal routine job, being solely due to air accidentally entering the hydraulic system. Fluid is virtually incompressible and it will therefore transmit pressure along a pipe. If there are air bubbles in the fluid, these will compress, giving a 'spongy' feeling to the brake pedal and making the brakes ineffective (see **FIG 4:65**).

Air may enter the system because the fluid level in the master cylinder reservoir has been allowed to drop too low. It may also enter because some part of the system has been disturbed. The other cause may be leaks, and if these are in the external pipework it may be possible to trace them and rectify the trouble. Try to locate these leaks by looking for fluid stains on the garage floor (see **FIG 4:66**). Leaks in the brake mechanism may also be due to defective seals or pipe lines. Any such failures must be rectified by a service station.

The method of eliminating air from the fluid is called 'bleeding' and this calls for the help of an assistant. **If the brakes continue to be ineffective after the operation, it is essential to have the system vetted by a service station. Never take chances with the braking system—your life may depend upon it.**

You will see in **Chapter 6, Section 6:13,** that the makers recommend a complete change of brake fluid and an examination of the system at specified intervals. These tasks are best left to a service station. Imminent failure of the braking system, particularly of the friction linings, the pipework and the hoses will certainly show up during an examination for an MOT Certificate.

Preliminaries to the operation:

The car must be raised on ramps or jacks, lifting first at the rear and then at the front. Do not get under the jacked-up car without using safety blocks (see **Section 2:2** in **Chapter 2**). If the tool kit jack is used, the correct sequence will involve extra work in moving the jack from side to side.

Buy a pint can of the correct brake fluid. This is Lockheed Disc Brake Fluid, Series 2. The only other fluid that is permissible is one conforming to Specification SAE.70R3. Your garage will advise you on this matter. **Never at any time introduce other types of fluid into the system and never use engine oil.** Be spotlessly clean when pouring fluid into the master cylinder reservoir. Dirt particles may cause complete brake failure. The reservoir is shown in **FIG 3:19.**

Explain to your assistant the necessity to keep the fluid level in the master cylinder reservoir above the halfway mark. If he looks into the reservoir after three or four brake pedal depressions he will be able to judge the need for topping up. **If the fluid falls** very low, air may enter the system and the whole operation will then have to be started again from scratch.

Arrange for signals to regulate the operation of the brake pedal. 'DOWN' calls for a full slow stroke of the pedal. 'HOLD' means holding the pedal in the down position. 'UP' is the call for releasing the pedal. When the pedal has returned to its released position it must be held there for a few seconds before another down stroke is attempted.

The equipment needed is a small ring spanner to fit the bleed screws and an 18 inch length of rubber or clear plastic tubing that will be a tight push fit on the bleed screw nipple (see **FIG 4:68**). The free end of the tube must be immersed in about $\frac{1}{2}$ inch of clean brake fluid in a clean glass container. **Do not use a milk bottle.**

The operation:

1 Start at one of the rear brakes. Identify the bleed screw as shown in **FIG 4:67** and clean off any dirt. Fit the ring spanner over the hexagon and push the tube over the nipple. The jar may stand on the ground or on a low box (see **FIG 4:68**).

2 Make sure that the master cylinder reservoir is full. Unscrew the bleed screw about half a turn and call 'DOWN'. Fluid level in the jar will rise and air bubbles may emerge from the immersed end of the tube. If clear plastic tubing is used, the air bubbles will be seen.

3 Call 'HOLD' and tighten the bleed screw. Call 'UP'. After the required wait of a few seconds, open the screw again and call 'DOWN'. Repeat the preceding instructions until there are no air bubbles emerging on a down stroke of the pedal. While the pedal is moving down, tighten the bleed screw moderately for the last time. **Do not overtighten it.** Check the fluid level in the master cylinder reservoir.

4 Repeat the operation on the second rear brake then move to the front brakes. When all four brakes have been bled, apply the pedal hard. It should feel solid. Any 'spongy' feeling means that air is still in the system and further bleeding will be required.

5 It will be tempting to use the extra fluid in the jar for topping-up. Resist this temptation, because the fluid will be aerated. **It really is the best plan to discard all such fluid.** If you are sure that the fluid is perfectly clean it may be used again, but not until after it has been standing for at least 24 hours. **Never leave fluid in an open jar because it will absorb moisture.** This could be dangerous.

6 There are devices advertised in motoring periodicals that eliminate the need for two-handed operation. It may be worthwhile to investigate these.

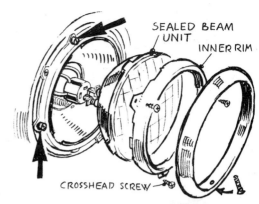

FIG 4:73 A sealed-beam headlamp dismantled. The beam adjusting screws are arrowed. They have slots and hexagonal heads

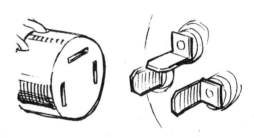

FIG 4:74 The headlamp wiring connector and the three contacts on the back of the light unit

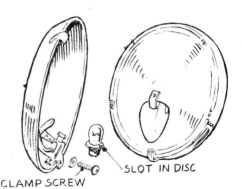

FIG 4:75 Dismantled foglamp on Princess cars. When fitting a bulb take care to align the slot

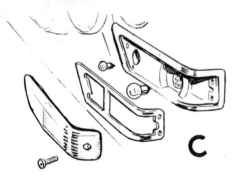

FIG 4:76 Gaining access to sidelamp and flasher bulbs on various models (see text)

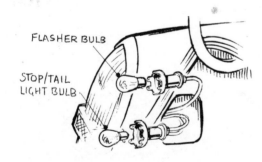

FLASHER BULB

STOP/TAIL
LIGHT BULB

FIG 4:77 On earlier models the lamp sockets must be removed for flasher and stop/tail lamp bulb renewal

THE CLUTCH

4:19 Adjusting the clutch stop

When the clutch pedal is depressed the clutch is operated hydraulically through its own master cylinder and piping to a slave cylinder. The master cylinder is under the bonnet adjacent to the brake master cylinder and is identified as the smaller of the two (see **FIG 4:69**). The slave cylinder is positioned on top of the flywheel housing (see **FIGS 3:19** and **4:70**). Its operation can be seen by asking somebody to depress the clutch pedal. As the pedal is depressed, fluid pressure forces out the slave cylinder piston and the piston pushrod. Movement of the pushrod operates a lever that disengages the clutch.

When the pedal is released this lever returns to a stop by the pull of a spring (see **FIG 4:70**). The stop is adjustable and is provided to allow a small amount of free movement in the clutch withdrawal mechanism. This free movement may be checked by pressing the clutch pedal with the fingers. The pedal should move freely at first before actual clutch withdrawal takes place. Check that you have this free movement.

As the clutch wears with use, this free movement diminishes. If there is no free play the clutch will slip and the engine will race without a corresponding urge from the transmission. Free play must be checked as follows:

Refer to **FIG 4:70** and pull the lever away from the engine as indicated by the top arrow. As the spring has a strong pull it may be advisable to get someone to help you.

With the lever pulled away from the stop, check the gap with your feeler gauges. A feeler 20 thousandths of an inch in thickness should be a smooth sliding fit. If the gap varies from this figure, slacken the locknut while holding the bolthead with a second spanner. Screw the bolt into the casing to increase the gap and unscrew it to reduce the gap (see **FIG 4:71**). Hold the bolthead while tightening the locknut and then recheck the gap.

4:20 Bleeding the clutch system

Bleeding the clutch system is exactly the same operation as that for bleeding the brakes (see **Section 4:18**). Refer to **FIG 4:72** for the location of the bleed screw. Make sure the clutch master cylinder is topped up with fluid. Use the same grade as that recommended for the brake system.

THE ELECTRICAL SYSTEM

4:21 Headlamp alignment regulations

The law requires car lighting to conform to certain standards and the most critical of these is headlamp beam setting. Although adjusting screws are provided (see **FIG 4:73**) it is not worth trying to set the beams yourself as it is difficult to do this accurately. Moreover, the car will not pass an MOT test unless the setting is correct. Garages use optical equipment for accurate setting.

The beam setting on a new car should be correct, but if you have bought a secondhand car on which previous owners have tried to adjust the beams, you may notice approaching cars flashing their headlights at you. This is generally a sign that your dipped headlamps are dazzling oncoming drivers. On the other hand, the beams may be so low or at such an angle that your vision is severly restricted. If you have any doubt about the headlamp setting and wish to stay on the right side of the law, have the setting checked as soon as possible.

4:22 Lamp and bulb renewal

Refer to the information in **Facts and Figures** for the types of bulbs that should be fitted when replacements are needed.

Headlamps:

Double-dipping, sealed-beam headlamps are fitted to all models. As there is no separate bulb, any failure of a filament calls for renewal of the complete unit (see **FIG 4:73**).

Removing the unit:

Remove the screw that retains the rim (see **FIG 4:73**). Ease the bottom of the rim forward with a screwdriver and then lift it off the lug at the top. Remove the three crosshead screws from the inner rim. Remove inner rim and sealed unit. Pull off wiring connector shown in **FIG 4:74**.

Make sure the lugs are correctly located when fitting a new unit. Engage the top lug of the outer rim and then turn the rim until the indicating pip is central. Press the lower part of the outer rim firmly into place and fit the retaining screw.

Fog lamps (Princess):

To renew the bulb, refer to **FIG 4:75** and remove the clamp screw and washer at the bottom of the rim. Prise the rim and glass off the body of the lamp, starting at the bottom and working towards the top locating lug.

Lift the retaining clip and remove the bulb. Fit the new bulb so that the slot in its disc engages with the projection in the holder. Hold the bulb with soft paper to avoid impairing the brilliance by finger marks. When fitting the rim, make sure the locating lug is properly retained before tightening the clamp screw.

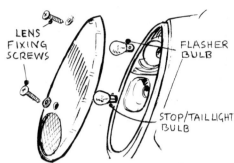

FIG 4:78 On Mk 2 models the lens is removed for access to the flasher and stop/tail lamp bulbs

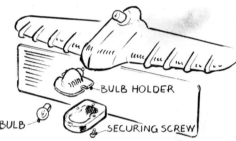

FIG 4:79 Earlier models have the number plate lamp incorporated in the boot lid motif

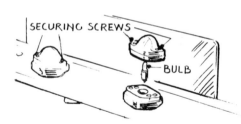

FIG 4:80 Some number plate lamps are mounted on the rear bumper. Remove the cover to reach the bulb

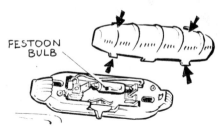

FIG 4:81 To renew the bulb of the interior light, remove the cover by gently squeezing at the points indicated

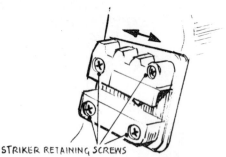

STRIKER RETAINING SCREWS

FIG 4:82 If a door does not latch properly try slackening the screws and moving the striker plate. Tighten the screws very securely after each adjustment

FIG 4:83 When a wheel is out of balance, weights are clipped to the rim to cure the trouble. Do not remove these weights

1mm

FIG 4:84 By law the depth of tread on a tyre must be not less than one millimetre at any point

FIG 4:85 Using a new 10p coin to check depth of tyre tread. If the dots round the coin rim are covered the depth is within the limit

Side lamps and flashers:

Austin, Morris, Wolseley and Riley:

Remove the two crosshead screws that secure the rim and lenses (see A in **FIG 4:76**). The bulbs are of the bayonet-fixing type and are taken out by pushing and turning them anticlockwise. Make sure the rubber gasket is replaced correctly.

Wolseley 1300 Mk 2:

A later modification incorporated three crosshead retaining screws directly into the lenses.

MG:

Refer to B in **FIG 4:76**. Press the cover and lens inwards and turn anticlockwise to release the retaining catches. Remove the bulbs as described for the Austin and other models.

Princess:

Remove the single crosshead screw at the side of the lens (see C in **FIG 4:76**) and lift off the rim and lens. The sidelight bulb is capless and can be pulled straight out of its holder. The flasher bulb is of the bayonet type and is removed by pushing it inwards and turning it anticlockwise.

Wing valance repeater lamps:

On many later models, repeater lamps are fitted on the sides of the wings. To remove the bulb, unscrew the single crosshead screw holding the lens. Some models have a capless-type bulb that can be pulled straight from its holder and others are fitted with a bayonet type of bulb.

Wolseley radiator badge light:

Lift the bonnet and feel behind the grille for the badge clips. Squeeze these together and push the badge forward. The bulb will now be accessible.

Tail/stoplights and rear flashing indicators:

Stop and tail lights have single bulbs, each with a double filament, the stoplight filament being more powerful. To ensure that the bulb is fitted correctly into its holder the bayonet pins are offset, which makes it impossible to fit the bulb the wrong way round. If difficulty is experienced in fitting the bulb, try turning it half a turn. The flasher bulb is of the normal bayonet type and is fitted in the ordinary way.

The bulbs on earlier models are reached from inside the luggage compartment, through openings in each side (see **FIG 4:77**). To remove the covering trim on MG, Riley and Wolseley models, lift the boot floor and pull out the spring clips. The bulb holders are a push fit. If they are tight, rock the holders and pull at the same time.

On later models:

The removal of the bulbs was simplified on later models as can be seen in **FIG 4:78**. Remove the two crosshead screws to release the lens.

On Countryman and Traveller cars:

The bulbs are removed through the openings in the sides of the luggage compartment as in **FIG 4:77**. The covering trim over the opening is held by three crosshead screws.

Number plate lights:

There are two possible locations for the number plate lamp(s). On some models it is under the motif on the boot lid (see **FIG 4:79**). On other models there may be a single or twin lamps on the rear bumper (see **FIG 4:80**).

Reversing lamp (Princess):

Undo the single screw securing the cover. Lift off the cover and glass and remove the bulb. The bulb has an ordinary bayonet fitting and may be replaced either way round.

Interior lamps:

The interior light operates automatically when one of the front doors is opened. It can also be operated from inside the car by an integral switch. To reach the festoon-type bulb on all models except the Princess gently squeeze and pull on the domed cover at the points indicated in **FIG 4:81**. On Princess models the cover is secured by two screws.

On both types the festoon bulb is simply sprung into position between two contacts.

Warning and panel lights:

On some models the bulb holders may be reached by feeling behind the facia panel. Be careful not to disturb the wiring.

The variations between later models are covered in **Section 7:15** under 'Flashers (direction indicators) faulty' (see **Solve-it-yourself**). The facia panel on De-luxe models may be lifted away after removing four screws (see **FIG 7:63**). Note that access is sometimes difficult.

BODYWORK

4:23 Adjusting door striker plates

The door striker plate illustrated in **FIG 4:82** can be moved slightly to compensate for wear. If the door rattles or lets in a draught the striker plate can be moved inwards by slackening the four crosshead screws, tapping the plate and then tightening the

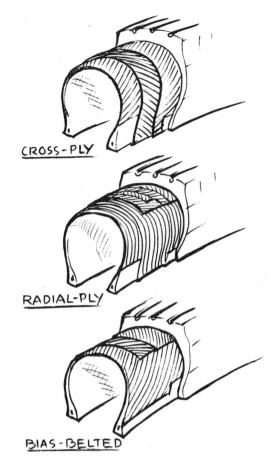

FIG 4:86   How the casing cords are disposed on the three types of tyre in general use

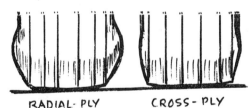

FIG 4:87   Although at the correct pressure, radial-ply tyres may look under-inflated due to the larger bulge where the tyre meets the road

FIG 4:88   Camber wear on tyres is generally due to accident damage or to wear of the steering or suspension systems

FIG 4:89   Irregular tyre wear may be due to a worn suspension system or to faults in the braking system

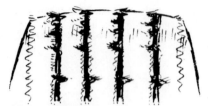

FIG 4:90   Tyre wear that produces a rasped or feathered appearance to the tread pattern is generally due to incorrect wheel tracking or to wheel misalignment

UNDER-INFLATION   OVER-INFLATION

FIG 4:91   How tread wear is affected by under- or over-inflation

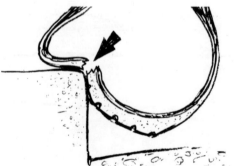

FIG 4:92   Driving over large sharp-cornered obstacles such as kerbstones may result in a fractured tyre casing

screws. Try the door to make sure it closes securely without slamming. Moving the plate slightly outwards will help if a door cannot be closed without unnecessary force. If you mark the outline of the plate on the door pillar before moving it, you can restore the plate to its original position if required.

WHEELS AND TYRES

4:24 The reason for wheel balancing

Unbalanced wheel assemblies are one of the main causes of abnormal wear of tyres and suspension parts, wheel wobble and vibration. If any one of these faults is apparent, have the wheels checked by a tyre specialist or a service station. Most of these operators have wheel balancing equipment which checks the wheel when it is mounted on the hub and running at high speeds. **Once wheels have been balanced on their hubs they should not be moved to another position unless there is no alternative. If a wheel is removed, mark it and refit it in the original position on the hub.**

During manufacture a tyre is balanced, but when it is fitted to a wheel and inflated the wheel and tyre assembly must be re-balanced. Even if the same tyre is removed and refitted to its original wheel the balance may be affected.

Balancing is effected by clipping small weights to the wheel rim. Removing or altering the position of weights may lead to serious imbalance (see **FIG 4:83**).

Another practice that may lead to imbalance is the repair of punctures by plugging tubeless cross-ply tyres. **Such a repair is only advisable in an emergency.** The tyre must then be repaired by vulcanising as soon as possible and the assembly re-balanced on the hub. **Never repair radial-ply tyres by means of plugs.**

4:25 Depth of tyre tread

It is against the law to run on defective tyres, and one of the requirements is a minimum depth of tread pattern (see **FIG 4:84**). There must be at least one millimetre depth of tread pattern around the circumference **and across three-quarters of the width.** To check this depth, small gauges are available from accessory shops. Another method is to use a new tenpenny piece. There is a raised rim around the face of the coin and inside the rim is a ring of small dots (see **FIG 4:85**). If the edge of the coin is positioned in the tread depressions and the dots are covered, the depth of tread at that point is within the limit. Try the test at several places.

4:26 Types of tyres

It is important that you should know which type of tyre is fitted to your car, both from the safety point of view and also because the law is very strict on the mixing of different tyre types.

There are three types of tyre in common use on private cars and they are known as cross-ply, radial-ply and bias-belted. These terms refer to the direction of the cords used in the tyre casing and the different cord patterns, which are illustrated in **FIG 4:86**, give very different running characteristics to the tyres. For this reason alone it would be unwise to use tyres of different construction on your car.

The law does not permit different types to be used on the same axle, nor does it allow radial-ply tyres to be used on the front wheels with cross-ply or bias-belted on the rear. If you **must** mix radial-ply with cross-ply tyres, the radials **must** be fitted to the rear wheels.

When you consider the confusion that could arise in the event of having to use the spare wheel it becomes obvious that the best course of action is to have all your tyres of the same type. In this way you will be safe and also complying with the law.

Identification of types:

High performance 1300 models are fitted with radial-ply tyres as standard equipment. Earlier 1100 Mk 1 and Mk 2 models were fitted with cross-ply tyres. To identify the type of tyres on your car, look at the markings on the sidewall. Note how the bulge helps when identifying tyres (see **FIG 4:87**).

Some tyres have the word RADIAL moulded on the sidewall or possibly the initials SR, HR or VR. In each case the R denotes 'Radial-ply'.

Normal cross-ply tyres have no identifying marks, but they show the size and some carry the initial S or H, which indicates that they are suitable for high speeds.

Bias-belted tyres carry the initials SB, HB or VB within the tyre size markings. The letter B denotes 'Bias-belted'.

Remoulds:

There are many remoulded tyres in use giving satisfactory service and they may be recognised by having the word REMOULD moulded into the sidewall. Remember that the safe speeds for these tyres are less than those for new tyres of similar type. Irrespective of the original rating of the tyre you should not exceed road speeds of more than 70 mile/hr.

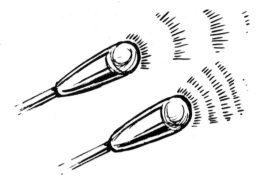

FIG 4:93 If the warning light of the direction indicators flashes more rapidly than usual it is generally a sign that an indicator (flasher) bulb has blown

FIG 4:94 Flexible brake hoses are subject to deterioration. Hose failure may lead to a total loss of braking

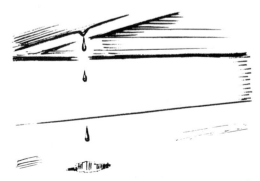

FIG 4:95 If loss of brake fluid is suspected, check the garage floor for stains due to leaks

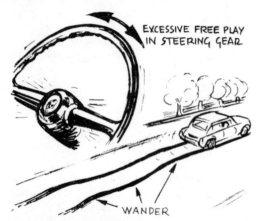

FIG 4:96   Excessive play in the steering gear may allow a car to wander dangerously

FIG 4:97   Tighten wheel nuts equally in the sequence 1, 3, 4, 2. Inset shows that tapered face of nut must contact wheel

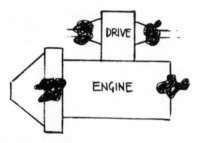

FIG 4:98   Looking down on the engine, this view shows the possible location of floor stains due to oil leaks from the drive shafts (top) and from the crankshaft (bottom)

4:27 Tyre defects and unusual tread wear

Irregular wear on the tread pattern of a tyre can give a good indication of the mechanical conditions of the brakes, steering and suspension. Irregular wear may also be due to neglected tyre pressures, fast cornering, heavy braking or rapid acceleration. Look for the following tread characteristics and take steps to remedy the suspected faults as soon as possible.

Camber wear:

This shows as severe wear on one side of the tread and may be on either shoulder (see **FIG 4:88**). Front tyres are more likely to show this characteristic than the rears, due to possible defects in the steering, but high speed cornering and suspension faults may also produce a similar effect.

Irregular wear:

The wear shown in **FIG 4:89** may be caused by worn bearings, grabbing brakes or badly adjusted brakes.

Misalignment wear:

Incorrect wheel alignment will cause a rasped and feathered edge on the tread pattern (see **FIG 4:90**). This may be attributed to incorrect tracking, worn bearings or unbalanced wheels. Incorrect tracking may be excessive toe-in or toe-out of the front wheels. Toe-in or toe-out means that the wheels are not parallel. For correct alignment the wheels must toe-out by $\frac{1}{16}$ inch. This must be checked by a dealer.

Wear due to under-inflation:

Under-inflation will cause excessive wear on the outside shoulders of the tyre (see **FIG 4:91**). It may also cause failure of the casing due to over-flexing of the walls. Check and inflate the tyres to the correct pressure. If you have been testing the pressures with your own gauge, check the gauge for accuracy. Do not forget that radial-ply tyres show a bulge that looks like under-inflation (see **FIG 4:87**).

Wear due to over-inflation:

Over-inflation leads to wear of the centre of the tread (see **FIG 4:91**). A hard tyre is more susceptible to impact fractures, and the result of this is described in the following paragraph. Make the same checks as described for under-inflated tyres.

Impact fractures:

Impact fractures are caused by driving over kerbs, or hitting potholes or hard objects in the road. This may result in a crack or split in the wall of the tyre (see **FIG 4:92**). Very often an impact fracture may not be obvious from the outside. Generally, however, there is a slight exterior bulge where the casing is fractured. As a safety precaution the tyre should be removed and examined (see 'Tyre defects' in the following Section).

DEFECTS

4:28 Dangerous defects

We are sure that our readers will appreciate some reference to those defects that are dangerous if neglected. These are most likely to show up in a car that has been bought secondhand, particularly if it has seen thousands of miles of service. Most of the defects will be spotted during an MOT test, but several months of daily use afterwards may cause any one of them to develop. **We would like to emphasise the need to rectify any such faults as soon as possible in the interests of safety.**

Flashers (direction indicators):

Apart from the occasional burned-out bulb, flasher systems give very little trouble. Because of this, drivers tend to assume that the system is working correctly. When the switch is operated, glance quickly at the green warning light before you alter direction. You will become used to the rate at which the mechanism clicks and the warning light flashes. Any rapid rise in the rate is usually due to failure of one of the flasher bulbs (see **FIG 4:93**). Operate the control and check all four lamps.

Renew a burned-out bulb as quickly as possible, meanwhile giving the appropriate hand signals and taking extra care at night.

If trouble does develop in the system, refer to **Chapter 7** for help in solving the problem.

Brakes pulling to one side:

This is due to unbalanced brakes and there are many causes (see **Chapter 7**). Do not drive the car with the brakes in this condition as faulty braking may pull the car into the opposite traffic lane or put the car into a dangerous skid.

Smooth pedal pads:

The pedal pads are grooved to prevent the foot slipping when pressure is applied. After much use the surface becomes smooth. If a driver then gets into the car with wet or muddy shoes and has to make a rapid stop or use the clutch, it is possible for his foot to slip off the pedal with disastrous results. The pads are renewable.

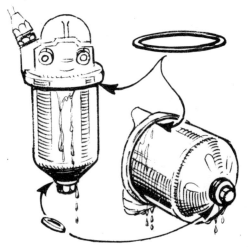

FIG 4:99 There may be a serious loss of engine oil if the gaskets for the oil filter head and fixing bolt are defective or not seating properly. Filter for cars with automatic transmission (right)

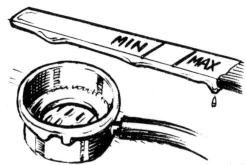

FIG 4:100 Loss of cooling water accompanied by rising level of engine oil are evidence of internal leakage of water into the engine

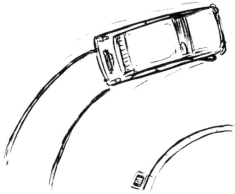

FIG 4:101 Excessive free play in the drive to the front wheels is most noticeable when turning on full lock

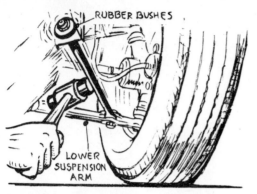

FIG 4:102 Gentle tapping with a soft-faced hammer may help to trace elusive rattles

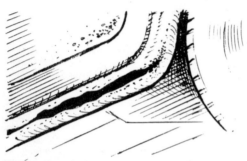

FIG 4:103 Corrosion has gone too far for simple cures when the bodywork is rotten and rust spots appear

Brake pipe corrosion:

The metal tubes which carry fluid to the brakes run along the underside of the car where there is every chance of serious corrosion. The pipes should be inspected at 12,000 mile intervals (see **Chapter 6**).

An MOT test will reveal rusted pipes, but if you have just bought a car that shows signs of body rust it is advisable to have the pipes checked at once. If corrosion causes a pipe to burst under braking pressure the brakes become useless just when they are most needed. Leaks may become apparent as stains on the garage floor and a continuous drop in the level of fluid in the master cylinder (see **FIG 4:95**). If the master cylinder requires frequent topping-up, refer to **Chapter 7**.

Flexible brake hoses:

There are four flexible hoses in the braking system (see **FIG 4:94**). These carry fluid from the metal pipes to the brakes. Hoses are subject to the usual deterioration of rubber and fabric. Inspect them at 12,000 mile intervals (see **Chapter 6**), but if loss of fluid is noticed at the master cylinder, refer to **Chapter 7**.

Brake fluid leaks:

A leak in the brake fluid circuit will eventually drain the master cylinder reservoir and cause a complete breakdown of the braking system. The leak may result from brake pipe or flexible hose failure, but refer to **Chapter 7** to make a complete check.

If you notice liquid stains on your garage floor or on any area over which the car has been parked, dip a finger into it and smell it. Brake fluid has a characteristic smell that is quite different from that of engine oil. Check against your can of brake fluid.

Steering play:

Play or wobble is transmitted to the driver through the steering wheel. Excessive play in the steering mechanism is revealed by the need for large movements of the steering wheel before the front wheels are deflected (see **FIG 4:96**). This gives rise to wander and the necessity for constant corrections by the driver. The inability to position the car accurately can be highly dangerous.

Wobble is transmitted to the steering wheel as a vibration. It may be due to out-of-balance wheel assemblies or to wear in hubs, drive shafts, and steering or suspension systems.

By referring to **Chapter 7** you will find instructions on tracing the fault, but rectification is a job for a garage.

Wheel nuts:

Loose wheelnuts will cause wheel wobble and may even lead to the loss of a wheel.

When replacing wheelnuts, make sure the tapered face of each nut is against the wheel (see **FIG 4:97**). Tighten them moderately at first in the order 1, 3, 4 and 2. Give them a final tighten in the same order when the wheel is on the road.

Check all wheelnuts before refitting the hub caps.

Tyre defects:

Section 4:27 covers these and also warns of the danger of mixing different types. An extremely dangerous situation may arise if a tyre suddenly deflates due to an impact fracture.

Jumping out of gear:

This is caused by wear in the gearbox, and usually happens when least expected. If you have engaged a lower gear to descend a steep hill or in order to overtake, it may be highly dangerous if you suddenly find yourself without any drive. Repairs to the gearbox may involve expensive removal of the power unit.

:29 Neglected defects may prove expensive

The stitch in time proverb applies equally well cars. This section will tell you how to trace efects and cure them before they become serious.

eaking engine oil:

Heavy oil consumption and patches of oil on the oor under the car show that the engine is in need of ttention (see **FIG 4:98**). However, the leaks may e due solely to defective joints and may be cheaply ured by tightening loose nuts or renewing gaskets.

If the leaks are at either end of the engine it is robable that the crankshaft seals are defective. here may also be leaks from the drive shaft seals. mall leaks may not necessarily need immediate ttention, but large pools of oil point to something eriously wrong. The possibility then exists of the ower unit running short of oil with unfortunate sults.

A continued glow from the amber oil pressure arning light when the engine is running is an dication that wear in the main and big-end earings may be contributing to a large drop in l pressure (see **Chapter 7**).

eaking filter gasket:

Oil leaking from the filter, either past the upper ealing gasket, or the washer under the bolt head ay lead to a serious loss of oil and possible seizure f the engine (see **FIG 4:99**). The glow from the nber warning light, indicating that the oil pressure as dropped, may not be timely enough to prevent e damage. If the filter has been disturbed (see ection 5:4 (8) in **Chapter 5**) always check the als after reassembly. Run the engine for a few inutes and check for leaks. Check again after riving for about a mile.

oss of water (coolant):

A water leak is indicated by the need for frequent pping up and/or tell-tale patches under the car. cure simple leaks, consult **Chapter 7**.

The need for frequent topping up without any utside indications of a leak is more serious, as this ill probably mean that water is getting into the ngine through a crack, or through a faulty cylinder ad gasket. An examination of the dipstick will nfirm this if it shows a muddy-looking emulsion f oil and water. It is also possible that the level will e over the full mark **and may even continue to se** (see **FIG 4:100**).

Another indication of such a leak is the condition of the water in the radiator. If there is oil on the surface and an oily smell (not to be confused with the smell of antifreeze) start the engine and check for bubbles. These will be a final confirmation.

The renewal of a faulty cylinder head gasket is a relatively inexpensive matter. Cracks are a serious problem and may prove expensive to cure.

The lubricating qualities of the oil will be seriously impaired by the presence of water and this will eventually lead to engine failure.

Expensive noises:

The car that produces an unusual noise is certain to start many arguments and some frustrating searches. However, if you are lucky enough to pinpoint the noise you may save yourself considerable expense by starting investigations at once.

Many noises are due to wear. For example, freeplay in the drive from the engine to the wheels will be heard (and felt) as a clonking, particularly when turning on full lock (see **FIG 4:101**). Once play is excessive it will rapidly become worse. The same applies to rattles that are heard when motoring. These may be due to wear in the suspension and steering systems or to something loose or rusted through in the exhaust system or engine mountings. Whatever the cause, it is worthwhile to trace and cure the defect as quickly as possible (see **FIG 4:102**).

Listen, too, for scraping sounds from the brakes. Friction pads that are down to the steel backing plate will cause rapid wear of the brake discs. Scraping may also be due to loose or worn hub bearings, and neglect to renew these may also involve the hub and disc.

Catching corrosion in time:

Once rusting has started on the bodywork, it will rapidly become worse. Corrosion may never be cured once it has begun, which is a good argument in favour of having a new car thoroughly rust-proofed at once (see **FIG 4:103**).

There is at least something the owner can do to beat the worst of the corrosion. One is to clean up the underside and apply a sealing compound. There are aerosol cans that make for easy application. There are also special compounds for spraying inside difficult places like doors and sills. These are advertised in motoring journals.

5

3000/6000 MILE SERVICE

5:1 Following the makers recommendations 5:2 Servicing at weekly intervals 5:3 Servicing at 3000 miles or 3 months 5:4 Servicing at 6000 miles or 6 months 5:5 Further checks

5:1 Following the makers recommendations

This chapter is based on the makers schedules, and is for the benefit of owners who prefer to service their cars at particular times or mileages.

At each 3000 mile interval the manufacturers give an alternative time of 3 months. For the motorist who does not complete such a mileage the time period will apply.

If your car has just been bought secondhand you may have no idea when it was last serviced. In this case the best plan is to start with the weekly service and work your way through all the other servicing instructions. You can then safely leave most of the items for another 3000 miles or 3 months, providing you still carry out the weekly checks.

If you carry out day to day servicing as suggested in **Chapter 3,** then continue with the long distance servicing, starting with **Section 5:3.**

5:2 Servicing at weekly intervals

1 Check the oil level (see **Chapter 3, Section 3:8**).
2 Test the tyre pressures (see **Chapter 3, Section 3:10**).
3 Check the battery electrolyte level (see **Chapter 3, Section 3:9**).
4 Check the wheel nuts for tightness (see **Chapter 4, Section 4:28**).

5:3 Servicing at 3000 miles or 3 months

(1) Topping up the carburetter piston damper(s)

Refer to **FIGS 3:19** and **4:8.** Unscrew the cap from the top of the suction chamber. Top up with engine oil (20W) to a level approximately $\frac{1}{2}$ inch above the piston rod. Do not overfill. If there is no vent hole in the screwed cap, the correct oil level is $\frac{1}{2}$ inch **below** the top of the piston rod.

(2) Checking the water level in the radiator: See Chapter 3, Section 3:8.

(3) Checking coolant level in expansion tank:

Refer to **FIG 3:10** to locate the tank. **Do not remove the cap while the system is hot.** Use an improvised dipstick to check the level. A depth of $2\frac{1}{4}$ inches of liquid will give the correct level. In winter, top up with neat antifreeze.

Take care not to mix the expansion tank and radiator caps. The cap for the expansion tank is fitted with a spring-loaded valve and is stamped with the figure 13. The plain radiator cap is shown in **FIG 3:9.**

(4) Topping up windscreen washer bottle:

The windscreen washer bottle is under the bonnet (see **FIG 3:19**). Unscrew the cap and lift the bottle

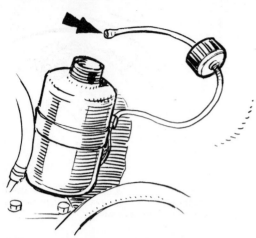

FIG 5:1 If the windscreen washer does not operate, check for a sticking valve in the suction tube (see arrow)

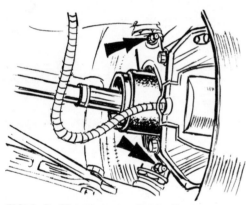

FIG 5:2 The arrows point to the two grease nipples on each steering swivel knuckle

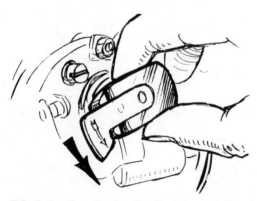

FIG 5:3 To check distributor centrifugal advance mechanism, turn rotor arm in direction of arrow and release it. Arm should return freely to original position

out of its bracket. Fill with clean water, adding a screen cleaning liquid if desired. **Do not add radiator antifreeze as this will damage the paintwork.**

If the washer does not work and everything else seems satisfactory, check the ball-valve at the bottom of the immersion tube, as it may be sticking (see **FIG 5:1**).

(5) Checking brake and clutch hydraulic reservoirs:

Raise the bonnet lid and refer to **FIG 3:19** to find the reservoirs. The brake reservoir is the larger of the two. Remove the two filler caps and check each fluid level. This should come to the base of the filler neck.

A small clean funnel is the best way of introducing fluid. **Use only the recommended fluid, which is Lockheed Disc Brake Fluid, Series 2 or Series 329. Be careful not to get the fluid on paintwork.**

(6) Checking and adjusting brakes:
See Chapter 4, Section 4:16.

(7) Inspecting brake lines and pipes:
See Chapter 4, Section 4:28 or Chapter 7, Section 7:14.

(8) Lubricating steering swivel knuckles:

Two lubricating nipples are provided on each steering swivel (see **FIG 5:2**). To ensure full penetration of grease, the front wheels should be jacked-up. Wipe the grease nipple before applying the gun. If the grease gun does not seal on the nipple, slip a piece of rag between the two. This will stop grease from exuding round the sides of the nipple.

(9) Additional checks:

During all 3000 mile inspections, include the four weekly checks. There are two remaining items to check before completing the schedule and both of these should be done by your local garage or service station.

1 Checking the tightness of the steering column clamp bolt.
2 Checking the headlamp beam setting.

5:4 Servicing at 6000 miles or 6 months

Complete all the 3000 mile inspections with the exception of the oil level check because the oil is now due for a change (see **Section 5:4 (7)**).

(1) Checking valve rocker clearances:
See Chapter 4, Section 4:14.

(2) Checking the fan belt tension:

See Chapter 4, Section 4:15.

(3) Checking and lubricating distributor:

To check the automatic advance mechanism, remove the distributor cover (see **Chapter 4, Section 4:9**). Turn the rotor arm in the direction of rotation. This is indicated by the arrow stamped on the brass segment. Release the arm. It should return to its original position without showing any tendency to stick (see **FIG 5:3**).

To check the vacuum advance mechanism, use a small screwdriver to push on the moving contact breaker plate (see **FIG 5:4**). Make sure the plate moves easily and smoothly. If any defect is shown in either of these tests, consult your garage.

Check the contact breaker points gap by referring to **Chapter 4, Section 4:9**.

Lubricate the cam bearing by removing the rotor arm. Add a few drops of oil down the spindle as shown in **FIG 5:5. Do not remove the screw inside the spindle.**

The automatic advance control is lubricated by dropping a few spots of oil down the space between the cam spindle and the contact breaker base plate (see **FIG 5:6**).

Apply a minute spot of oil to the contact breaker pivot and a thin smear of grease on the cams. **Do not over-oil, or allow oil and grease to get onto the contacts.**

(4) Cleaning and adjusting sparking plugs:

See Chapter 4, Section 4:12.

(5) Checking and adjusting clutch return stop:

See Chapter 4, Section 4:19.

(6) Inspecting front brake pads for equal wear:

See Chapter 4, Section 4:16.

(7) Draining and refilling engine oil:

The drain plug is on the righthand side of the transmission casing (see **FIG 5:7**), underneath the engine.

Engine oil changes should be made whilst the engine is still warm because then the oil is thinner. When the plug has been removed, allow at least 10 minutes for the oil to drain.

The drain plug is magnetic and you will find bits of swarf sticking to it. Clean it by wiping with non-fluffy cloth. The copper sealing washer should be renewed at alternate oil changes (see **FIG 5:8**).

Refit the drain plug and washer, tightening thoroughly. Remove the rocker cover filler cap (see **FIG 3:19**) and pour in an approved grade of oil until the level reaches the MAX mark on the dipstick (see

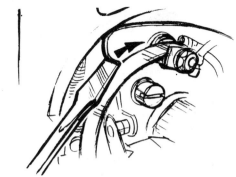

FIG 5:4 To check that distributor vacuum advance mechanism moves freely, push on the moving contact plate as shown

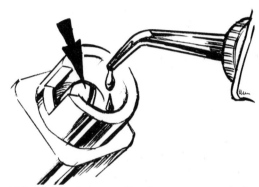

FIG 5:5 Lubricate distributor cam spindle with a few drops of oil as shown. Do not remove the central screw (see arrow)

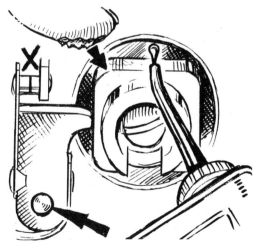

FIG 5:6 Lubricating the advance mechanism and applying grease to the distributor cams (top). Apply one tiny spot of oil to contact breaker pivot (bottom arrow). Keep grease and oil off contacts at X

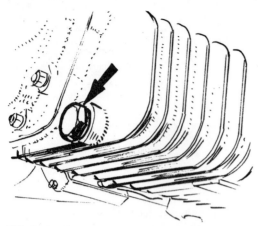

FIG 5:7 The engine and transmission drain plug is underneath, on the righthand side

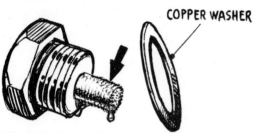

COPPER WASHER

FIG 5:8 Clean the magnet of the drain plug free from steel particles. The sealing washer must be in good condition.

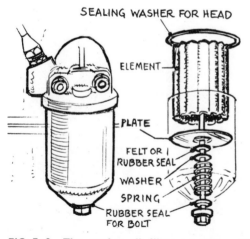

SEALING WASHER FOR HEAD

ELEMENT

PLATE

FELT OR RUBBER SEAL

WASHER

SPRING

RUBBER SEAL FOR BOLT

FIG 5:9 The engine oil filter on cars with manual gearchange. Note correct assembly of parts inside bowl. Filter location is shown in FIG 3:19

FIGS 3:7 and **3:8**). On cars with manual gearchange, add $8\frac{1}{2}$ pints of oil. On cars fitted with automatic transmission, add 9 pints of oil. Both these figures apply if the oil filter element has not been changed. If it has, in each case add an extra pint.

Run the engine for at least 2 minutes to recharge the filter case and then stop it and let it stand for a few minutes before checking the level again.

(8) Fitting a new oil filter element:

Cars with manual gearchange:

Whenever the oil is changed a new filter element should be fitted. First of all, disconnect the battery if a warning light is fitted. Refer to **FIG 5:9** and from underneath the car unscrew the $\frac{9}{16}$ inch AF bolt. As the bowl breaks away from the filter head oil will run out, so have a container handy to catch it. Pull the bowl downwards and manoeuvre it past the engine sump. Remove the old element and scrap it. Clean the rest of the parts in solvent and wipe dry.

Check that the inner rubber or felt seal is a tight fit on the bolt, otherwise oil will bypass the element. The large rubber seal which fits in a groove in the filter head must be renewed at the same time as the element. Prise out the old seal but take care not to damage the groove.

Do not try to work the new seal into the groove from one point only or you will finish with a surplus loop. The correct way is to dip the ring in brake fluid or smear it with rubber grease and press it into the groove at four points equally spaced. Continue pressing in short sections (see **FIG 5:10**).

To reassemble, insert the centre bolt, making sure the seal is between the head and the bowl. Working inside the filter bowl, fit the spring and steel washer over the bolt. Follow these with the felt or rubber ring. Insert the filter plate and finally the new filter element. Locate the bowl in the filter head and tighten the centre bolt. Check that the bowl is pressing on the seal correctly. To ensure a good seal turn the bowl to and fro before the bolt is fully tightened. Do not over-tighten or the seal may be damaged and the bowl distorted.

Read the previous section regarding filling up with oil. Reconnect the battery, start the engine and check for leaks. **This check is most important.** Running the fingers round the bowl and the fixing bolt will quickly detect leaking oil. Stop the engine to make this examination.

Cars with automatic transmission:

To remove the filter bowl, refer to **FIG 5:11**. Place a container under the filter to catch draining oil. Slacken the clamp bolt of the ignition coil mounting bracket and reposition the clamp to give a clear passage for the filter bowl. Using a socket or box spanner inserted through the hole in the engine mounting plate, unscrew the centre bolt. As there are two different lengths of element in service, make sure the new one is of the correct type.

All other details are the same as those given for the filter fitted to manual gearchange models.

Replace the filter. After completion, readjust and tighten the coil mounting bracket.

(9) Oiling door locks and hinges:

Pump a few spots of oil through the small hole in the door lock (see **FIG 5:12**) and around the door hinges (see **Section 7:17**). Wipe away surplus oil to prevent it getting on clothing.

Apply oil to the bonnet and boot lid hinges, the support catches and the bonnet lid catch.

(10) Lubricating the generator bearing:

Add two or three drops of engine oil to the generator bearing. **Do not over-oil.** Access is through the central hole in the rear end bearing plate, as shown in **FIG 5:13**. The alternator shown in **FIG 7:56** does not need periodical lubrication.

(11) Checking the lights:

Check all lamps to see that they function correctly. Get someone to depress the brake pedal with the ignition switched on to see if the rear stoplights are working. It is also possible to carry out a single-handed check by watching for the illumination inside a darkened garage.

(12) Checking the condition of the battery:

There are two ways to do this. One is to ask a service station to connect a high-discharge meter across the cells. This will reveal those that are defective. The other is to check the specific gravity of the electrolyte (the battery acid) with an hydrometer.

Hydrometers are available at accessory shops. Use as shown in **FIG 5:14**. Before checking, top-up the electrolyte level (see **Section 3:9, Chapter 3**) and go for a short run to disperse the distilled water. Insert the hydrometer tube and suck up electrolyte by squeezing and releasing the rubber bulb. When the float is raised, read off the level of the liquid on the scale. This reading is the specific gravity of the electrolyte as can be seen in the inset at the top of the illustration.

The figure obtained will indicate the state of charge of the battery in the following way:

Specific gravity 1.27 to 1.29 . . Cell fully charged
Specific gravity 1.19 to 1.21 . . Cell half-charged
Specific gravity 1.11 to 1.13 . . Cell discharged

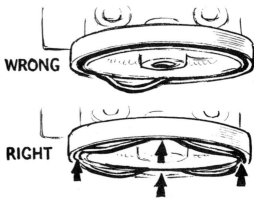

FIG 5:10 When fitting the filter head seal, take care not to finish with a surplus loop (top view). The best way to fit the seal is to press it in at four equidistant points (lower view)

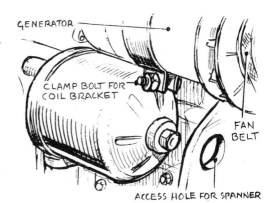

FIG 5:11 On cars with automatic transmission, access to the oil filter bolt is through the hole indicated. Before the bowl can be removed, the coil bracket must be moved

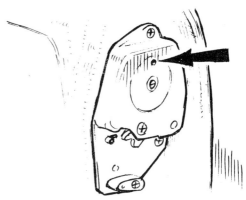

FIG 5:12 Location of lubricating hole in door lock. Due to variations in locks, the position may differ slightly

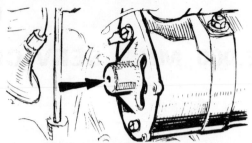

FIG 5:13 Location of lubricating hole for end bearing of generator

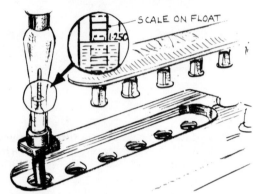

FIG 5:14 Checking the specific gravity of battery electrolyte (acid), using an hydrometer. The inset shows the graduations on the float

If there are marked variations between the battery cells it is likely that there is a fault somewhere. **Do not try to rectify the condition by adding neat sulphuric acid.**

The temperature of the electrolyte has a bearing on the figures for specific gravity just given. If it is around the normal room temperature of 60°F (16°C) the figure will apply. If the temperature is above that, add .002 to the specific gravity reading for each 5°F (3°C) rise. If the temperature is below, subtract .002 for the same drop.

If a battery becomes fully discharged, have it recharged at once. **It will be ruined if left in the fully discharged condition.**

5:5 Further checks

Apart from the servicing covered in this chapter, the maker's schedule calls for two further checks at 6000 miles. Normally these are not checks that an owner is equipped to carry out.

The first is a check of the front wheel alignment. The effect of misalignment is given in **Section 4:27**, in the preceding chapter. Checking should be carried out by a garage.

The second check, which should also be entrusted to a garage, is on the condition and security of the suspension units and the front drive universal joints.

6

12,000 MILE SERVICE

:1 Service routine at 12,000 miles or 12 months

To carry out this service, complete all the 6000 mile checks in **Chapter 5** except for cleaning and adjusting the sparking plugs. Then do the following:

:2 Fit new sparking plugs

See **Chapter 4, FIG 4:40.**

:3 Fit new air filter element(s)

In **FIGS 6:1, 6:2** and **6:3** three different air filters are shown. Refer to the one appropriate to your car and read the following instructions:

Single small element:

1 Refer to **FIG 6:1,** unscrew the single wing nut and lift off the cover.
2 Remove the element and scrap it. It is not possible to clean it. Wipe the inside of the element casing. Keep all dust out of the carburetter intake.
3 Fit a new element and replace the cover.

Single, large element:

1 Refer to **FIG 6:2.** This filter assembly may be made of plastic. Earlier types were of metal.
2 Remove the two wing nuts and lift the complete assembly off the carburetter.

3 Lift off the top cover. The plastic type will require prising off with a screwdriver placed in the slots. Remove the filter element and wipe the inside of the casing. Discard the old element.
4 Fit a new element and replace the cover. Make sure the arrow on the cover is aligned with the lug on the container and the seal between the casing and carburetter is positioned correctly.
5 On the single HS4 carburetter fitted to cars with automatic transmission, check that both internal O-rings are correctly positioned.
6 Refit the filter assembly and tighten the wing nuts.

Double, small element:

1 Refer to **FIG 6:3** and unscrew the two wing nuts, remove the washers and the filter cover.
2 Lift out both elements and discard them.
3 Wipe the inside of the casing clean and fit the new elements. Refit the cover and tighten the wing nuts.

6:4 Fitting new oil filler cap when it incorporates a filter

An air filter is incorporated in the oil filler cap on all models that are equipped with closed circuit breathing (see **FIG 6:4**). This filter eventually becomes blocked and the whole cap assembly must then be renewed. Do not attempt to clean the cap and filter.

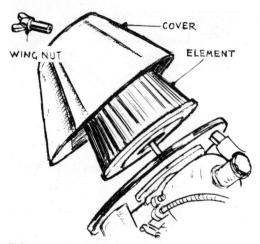

FIG 6:1 The earlier type of air cleaner with metal casing and single small element

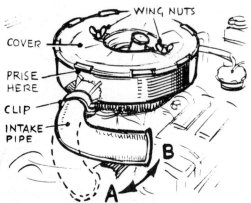

FIG 6:2 Single air cleaner with large element. If made of plastic, prise off cover at slots

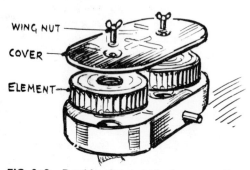

FIG 6:3 Double-element air cleaner as fitted to some twin-carburetter engines

6:5 Cleaning breather control valve

Refer to **FIG 6:4** to service the valve.

1 Remove the spring clip and dismantle the valve.
2 Clean all the metal parts with petrol, but clean the diaphragm in a strong detergent or methylated spirits.
3 If the deposits are difficult to remove, do not use abrasives but immerse the parts in boiling water before washing them in petrol.
4 Reassemble the valve, taking care that the metering needle is seated correctly in the cruciform guides and the diaphragm is the right way round, so check the illustration. Run the engine at idling speed and remove the oil filler cap. Engine speed should rise by about 200 rev/min if the valve is working. This is a good method of checking valve operation.
5 If parts of the valve are worn, new ones must be fitted. Early-type valves without the cruciform guides are an assembly and need complete renewal.

Servicing breather on 1275 cc engines:

On 1275 cc engines that are not fitted with the preceding type of control valve, a combined breather and oil separator is fitted to the flywheel housing (see inset, bottom right in **FIG 6:4**).

To remove the filter, pull off the detachable cap and extract the wire gauze. Wash the gauze and the cap in petrol before reassembling and replacing.

6:6 Examining steering gaiters and ball joints

The steering gear is bolted to the bulkhead low down behind the engine. It is readily seen if the front wheels are removed. At each end of the steering housing there are rubber bellows-type gaiters (see **FIG 6:5**). If these are split or damaged, oil will leak out and dirt may find its way in. It is essential to have defective gaiters renewed and fresh lubricant introduced after the mechanism has been cleaned and examined.

There are rubber boots that seal the outer ball joints of the steering linkage (see **FIG 6:6**). These are visible if the front wheels are removed. If the boots are found to be damaged, dirt may have entered the ball joints. This will lead to rapid wear. The only cure is to have new joints fitted.

6:7 Checking suspension and steering

This is a job for a garage, as the suspension pressure should also be checked. It is possible to make one or two simple but reasonably effective checks yourself without special equipment.

Checking suspension trim:

The hydrolastic suspension system is pressurized, and this pressure controls the attitude of the car. If there has been any loss of pressure on one side of the car, that side will settle and the car will look lop-sided.

The makers have given dimensions for the height of the wing arch from the centre of each wheel. These dimensions for the various models will be found in **Facts and Figures**.

To check, stand the unladen car on level ground. It must be in running trim with 4 gallons of fuel in the tank. Measure from each wheel centre to the under-side of the wheel arch as shown in **FIG 6:7**. Mark the wheel cap centrally by measurement. A strip of paper that is the diameter of the cap may be folded in half and used to find the centre. Note that there is $\frac{1}{4}$ inch tolerance each way on the specified height.

If the measurements are not within the tolerance, the car must be re-pressurized by a dealer. Accidental loss of fluid in the system will allow the car to settle lower than usual. **In this condition it may safely be driven to a service station if road speed does not exceed 30 mile/hr.**

Checking the steering:

Hold the steering wheel with two fingers and a thumb. Gently work the wheel backwards and forwards to determine the amount of free play. This is the total movement before resistance is felt. Any movement over $1\frac{1}{2}$ inches will indicate excessive wear in the steering mechanism (see **FIG 6:8**).

Checking the hub bearings and swivel hubs for wear:

With the front wheels raised, lift one of the wheels up and down by placing a bar under the tyre (see **FIG 6:9**). Any play here will suggest that either the swivel hub ball joints or the wheel bearings are worn.

By grasping the tyre horizontally and rocking the wheel back and forth, free play due to wear in the linkages can be detected (see **FIG 7:49**). **This action must not cause violent reversals of the steering gear or damage may result.** Undue free play is a job for your garage.

6:8 Renewing wiper blades

Pull the arm away from the windscreen. To remove the blade from the arm, pull the top of the blade towards the front of the car and withdraw it gently from the arm with a curving pull. Later types are pressed on and held by a spring clip (see **FIG 6:10**).

To remove the blade rubber, depress the retaining pin or rubber key on the outer end of the blade and slide the rubber out of the clip. Renew blades every year.

Repositioning wiper arm:

Refer to **FIG 6:11** and use a small screwdriver to lift the spring clip out of the retaining groove.

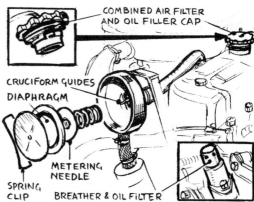

FIG 6:4 Later type of breather control valve parts. Inset (top left) shows the filler cap that incorporates an air filter. On 1275 cc engines without control valve there is a breather and oil filter on the flywheel housing (bottom right)

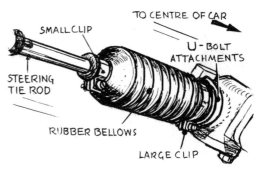

FIG 6:5 The rubber bellows at each end of the steering gear must be sound. Cracks or damage may lead to loss of lubricant and entry of dirt

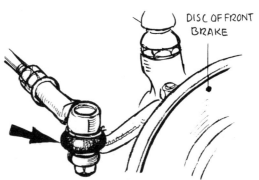

FIG 6:6 The rubber boot on the outer ball joint of each steering tie rod must be without cracks or damage

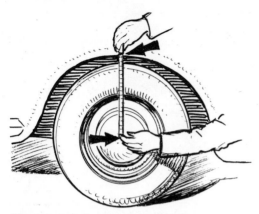

FIG 6:7 Measuring trim height from wheel centre to underside of wheel arch. Used as a check on correct setting of suspension system

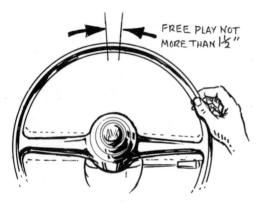

FREE PLAY NOT MORE THAN 1½"

FIG 6:8 Checking the free play in the steering gear. Use light finger pressure only

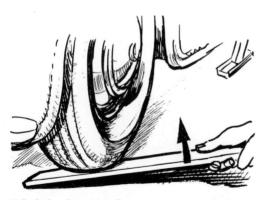

FIG 6:9 Checking for wear in the swivel hub ball joints or wheel bearings

Withdraw the arm and then reposition it. Push it home on the spindle so that it is secured by the retaining clip. Check the action, **but make the screen wet before doing so.**

6:9 Lubricating the water pump (early models only)

If the pump has a screw into the body, as shown in **FIG 6:12**, remove the screw and press some grease into the hole with a finger. A volume of grease equal to that of the screw will be sufficient. Refit the screw. **Do not try to force grease into the hole with a grease gun. Excessive grease will ruin the water seal.**

6:10 Checking for brake fluid leaks

The need for constant topping up of the master cylinder fluid is a sure sign that there is a leak somewhere (see **Chapter 4, Section 4:28**). Take immediate advice from your service station.

To minimize the risk of a leak developing unnoticed, the pipe lines, wheel cylinders and master cylinders should be checked at the specified mileages, or after the lapse of 1 year, whichever is the sooner. If you make the checks yourself, you will have to work under the car, so make sure any jacks and supports are firmly placed (see **Chapter 2, Section 2:2**).

Chock those wheels that touch the ground and release the handbrake. Get an assistant to press down hard on the brake pedal while you proceed with the inspection. Start with the pipes and unions adjacent to the master cylinder (see **FIG 3:19**) and work your way through the system until you reach the points where the flexible hoses are attached to the brakes (see **FIG 4:94**). Look for the signs of fluid leakage at the lower end of the master cylinder, in the region of the front brake pads and from the drums and backplates of the rear brakes (see **FIGS 4:57, 4:58** and **4:67**).

Corrosion of metal brake pipes may be serious, and is generally found to be worse towards the rear of the car (see **FIGS 4:66** and **4:95**). An elderly secondhand car ought to be checked at once for such corrosion and for defective hoses. **Never take a chance on possible brake failure.**

6:11 Draining and flushing radiator

Two draining points are provided on earlier cars for emptying the cooling system. There is one under the radiator bottom tank as shown in **FIG 6:13** and another at the rear of the cylinder block (see **FIG 6:14**). Access to the radiator plug is from underneath the car.

Remove both these drain plugs and if the car is equipped with a heater, move the heater lever inside the car to the MAX position. Remove the radiator filler cap. If necessary, keep antifreeze solution for use again. If the radiator has no drain plug, release the bottom hose from the radiator (see **FIG 6:15**).

The system must be flushed through with clean water by inserting a hose in the radiator filler neck. Flush until the water runs clear. Alternatively use cans of water.

If there has been trouble with overheating, try clearing the deposits with one of the proprietary radiator compounds.

Refilling the system:

Refit the drain plugs or reconnect the bottom hose. If antifreeze is being added, refer to the next Section.

If the car is not fitted with a heater, pour clean water into the radiator until it reaches the bottom of the filler neck.

If a heater is fitted, move the heater lever to the MIN position. Disconnect the heater hose (see **FIG 6:16**). Insert a funnel into the hose and fill the system through the funnel. Leave the radiator cap off and fill to the base of the radiator filler neck.

Check the level in the expansion tank (see **Section 5:3 (3)** in **Chapter 5**). Refit the radiator and expansion tank caps, taking care not to mix them (see **FIG 3:9**). Reconnect the heater hose and move the interior lever to the MAX position. Start the engine and run it up to normal working temperature. **Do not remove the filler caps whilst the system is hot.** Allow the engine to cool and then check the level in the radiator. Top up if necessary.

6:12 Using antifreeze in the cooling system

To prevent the cooling system freezing it is necessary to add antifreeze to the water. **This is essential if a heater is fitted, because the heater cannot be drained.**

Before adding antifreeze it is essential to cure any leaks in the system. If there is a leak, constant topping up with water will dilute the mixture and reduce the degree of protection. Check the hoses and renew them if they have obviously deteriorated. Some clips are extremely difficult to get at and in this case it would be better to ask your garage to fit the new hoses.

Leaks are always aggravated when antifreeze is added, so check as thoroughly as possible.

The cooling system, with a heater fitted, holds 6¾ pints of water, one pint of this being contained in the heater. However, as the heater cannot be drained the volume of antifreeze and water will be 5¾ pints. There are many types of antifreeze mixtures available. Buy one that carries the specification BS3151 or BS3152 as it will contain a corrosion inhibitor.

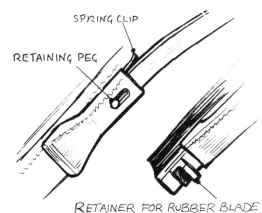

FIG 6:10 Later type of wiper blade fixings. Blade to arm (left), rubber to blade (right)

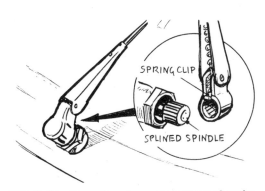

FIG 6:11 How the wiper arm is secured to the spindle. Note adjustment splines for altering position

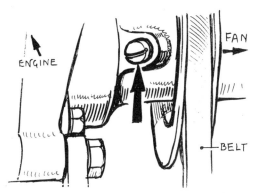

FIG 6:12 Early models may have provision for lubricating the water pump bearings. Remove the screw to introduce grease.

FIG 6:13 The drain plug in the bottom tank of the radiator. Later models may have no plug (refer to FIG 6:15)

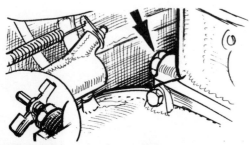

FIG 6:14 The cylinder block drain plug is behind the engine. Some models have a tap instead (left)

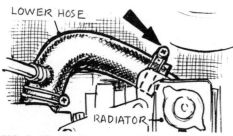

FIG 6:15 On later models without a radiator drain plug, release the bottom hose, to empty the radiator

FIG 6:16 Disconnect the heater hose, insert a funnel and use it to refill the cooling system when a heater is fitted

The amount of protection from frost will depend on how much antifreeze you use. The following table is a guide.

Antifreeze	Commences freezing at	Frozen solid at
1½ pints	—13°C (9°F)	—26°C (—15°F)
2¼ pints	—19°C (—2°F)	—36°C (—33°F)
3¼ pints	—36°C (—33°F)	—48°C (—53°F)

Two pints would give adequate protection in the South and West. To be on the safe side, three pints would be complete protection.

Before adding the antifreeze, replace the drain plugs. Remove the cap on the expansion chamber and pour in approximately a ¼ pint of neat antifreeze (see FIG 3:10). Replace the cap.

Refer now to Section 6:11 and refill the system, pouring the antifreeze in first. Be careful not to splash it about as antifreeze will damage the paintwork. Any splashes on the bodywork should be washed off immediately.

Because of its adverse effect on the paintwork, antifreeze must not be used in the windscreen washer bottle. De-icing fluids that are specially made for windscreen washers are available.

Antifreeze can remain in the cooling system for two years, but make sure that in the second winter the solution is strengthened by adding more antifreeze. If you are not sure about it, your garage can measure the specific gravity of the mixture and tell how much more antifreeze is needed to bring it up to full strength.

After the second winter, drain and flush the system and fill with fresh antifreeze solution.

6:13 Extended period for brake servicing

In addition to the normal periodic servicing, the makers recommend the following preventative maintenance:

1 Change all the brake fluid in the system every 18 months or 24,000 miles, whichever is the sooner.
2 Examine, and if necessary renew all hydraulic seals and flexible hoses every 3 years or 40,000 miles, whichever is the sooner. At the same time examine the internal working surfaces of hydraulic parts and renew those that are worn or corroded.

Both operations must be carried out by a competent service station. If the car is secondhand or over three years old, carry out the checks unless there is positive proof that it is unnecessary.

SOLVE IT YOURSELF

7:1 Keeping the wheels turning

When you buy a new car you can reasonably expect it to give you a long period of trouble-free motoring. On the other hand, a well-used car that has been running for thousands of miles will be affected by wear and deterioration. These will give rise to problems that this chapter should help you to solve.

When domestic gadgets become faulty they are usually given to experts for diagnosis and repair, and some delay while this is being done can often be tolerated. Unfortunately, trouble with the car may happen at a most inconvenient time when the owner would give anything to be able to get motoring again. The object of this chapter is to provide him with a series of logical checks that will help him to pinpoint, and in most cases, cure the trouble in the speediest manner.

The checks are set out in diagrammatical sequences like those to be seen in **FIGS 7:4** and **7:5**. Each check is fully explained in an appropriate Section in the text. We propose to deal with engine trouble first.

Notice how checks A, B, C and D in **FIG 7:4** are amplified in **FIGS 7:5, 7:14, 7:21** and **7:25**. The numbered checks in each of these are indicated in the text by numbers in brackets thus (1), (2) and so on.

7:2 What to do when the engine gives trouble

Apart from defects elsewhere in the car, the worst things that can happen to you are that the engine will not start or that it fails while you are on the road. **FIG 7:1** shows that an engine depends upon several systems for correct functioning, and trouble may occur in any one of them. This chapter will deal with each problem in turn.

Before making a start, we would like to point out the value of being able to describe how an engine fails, if it does so while you are actually motoring. For example, it may start to misfire spasmodically until it eventually stops. This is most likely to be fuel trouble. If the engine starts readily enough after a short wait it is almost certainly due to intermittent failure in the fuel supply.

On the other hand, if the engine cuts out dead, the trouble is most likely to be in the ignition system.

Engine trouble that is accompanied by strange mechanical noises is covered in **Section 7:6**.

When you are bothered by unusual sounds, it is worthwhile to ask a knowledgeable friend to sit in the passengers seat. Noises that seem to the driver to be coming from his side of the car are frequently traceable to the passengers side, so elusive are they.

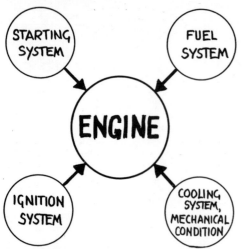

FIG 7:1 The systems upon which the engine depends for correct functioning

FIG 7:2 If the engine will not start, check that the ignition warning light glows and that there is ample fuel

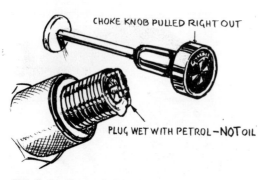

CHOKE KNOB PULLED RIGHT OUT

PLUG WET WITH PETROL—NOT OIL

FIG 7:3 Over-choking is a common cause of difficult starting. The sparking plugs may be shorted with petrol

7:3 Preliminary checks if engine fails to start

Assuming that the engine will not start, the first things to do are to check that the ignition light glows and that the fuel gauge indicates when the key is turned. The starter must turn the engine briskly. The other essential check is to be quite certain that there is petrol in the tank. This sounds like a joke, but an empty tank as the cause of non-starting has been with us since the beginning of motoring!

If you are satisfied that fuel is there, continue with the checks indicated in FIG 7:4. However, before setting out on these, it is advisable to check for over-choking.

Over-choking:

Prolonged use of the choke may lead to excessive fuel in the engine system. This may be seen as wetness of the sparking plug points accompanied by a smell of petrol (see FIG 7:3). The smell of petrol may be strong when the bonnet is raised.

If the starter continues to turn the engine at a good speed, operate it with the choke knob pushed right in and the accelerator pedal pressed to the floor. If the engine then fires spasmodically, ease back on the pedal to induce the engine to run faster without it dying out. It may be necessary to use a little choke in order to keep it running. If over-choking was the cause of non-starting, some revving of the engine will quickly clear it. **Never use the choke when trying to start a hot engine.**

A quick visual check:

While the bonnet is raised and before tackling the checks suggested in FIG 7:4, take a quick look round at all the electrical connections to the distributor and coil, particularly if the starter motor works well. The locations are shown in FIG 3:19. A disconnected wire may be all that is wrong. If there is nothing obviously at fault proceed with the sequence of checks.

7:4 The engine will not start

Reference to FIG 7:4 will show that there are four likely causes of trouble, A, B, C and D. We will take the starter first because most of the checks are simple to make. Refer to FIG 7:5.

A—Check the starting system:

Before working on the electrical side of the starting system we must emphasise the need for care when checking the heavy cables that carry current to the motor. **Do not use a screwdriver or spanner on the terminals without disconnecting the battery.** Shortcircuiting will lead to violent sparking and may even burn the operator.

It will be useful to know that there is a hand-operated starter switch under the bonnet. This is located on the wing behind the battery (see **FIG 7:6**). To operate the starter motor, press the rubber-covered knob firmly upwards. **Keep away from the fan while doing this and make sure the gear-lever is in neutral, with the handbrake applied.**

(1) Starter makes no sound:

If the starter does not operate, switch on the headlamps and get someone to watch them while you turn the ignition key. If the lights go dim and then brighten again when the key is turned off, this indicates that the starter motor is jammed or faulty. If the lights are already dim, there is a fault in the electrical supply. If the lights remain bright, there is a breakdown in the electrical system to the starter.

If a jammed starter motor is suspected:

FIG 7:7 shows the outer end of the starter motor shaft. This is squared to take a spanner. Switch off the ignition and turn the shaft to and fro until it comes free. The motor should then run normally. If it does not, then try the other checks where they apply. The motor is low down in front of the engine, below the distributor (see **FIG 3:19**).

Another method that will free a jammed starter motor on cars with manual gearchange is to engage top gear. **Make sure the ignition is switched off.** Push the car backwards and forwards. This should free the jammed pinion and will be felt as a sudden release of excessive resistance. **Do not try this method if the car is on a steep hill.**

If the electrical supply seems faulty:

When switched on, the headlamps may be dim and the starter motor run slowly or not at all. This points to failure of the battery or the electrical connections. If the battery has performed well until now and has not been left idle for a long period, check the terminal connections. Loose connections become hot after attempts to start. Remove the cable connectors, and scrape the battery posts and the inner surfaces of the connectors clean and bright (see **FIG 7:8**). Refit the connectors. **Tighten the screws only moderately or the threads will be stripped.** If this happens try a fatter screw or even a woodscrew at a pinch. Make sure the battery earth connection to the car body is clean and secure (see **FIG 7:9**). Now try the starter again. If there is no improvement, check all the cables and connections between the battery, the starter solenoid switch (see **FIG 7:6**) and the starter. Make sure all nuts are tight, but do not overtighten them. Hold cables still while turning the nuts. If there is no improvement, have the battery recharged and check the starter motor as instructed later.

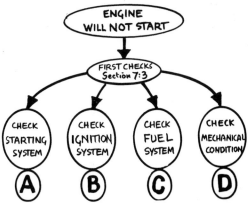

FIG 7:4 The systems to be checked when the engine will not start

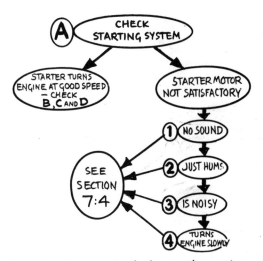

FIG 7:5 How to check the starting system. Items 1, 2, 3 and 4 are discussed in Section 7:4

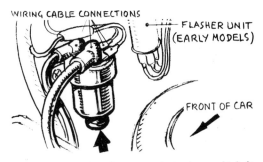

FIG 7:6 The hand-operated starter switch is just behind the battery. Press the knob upwards

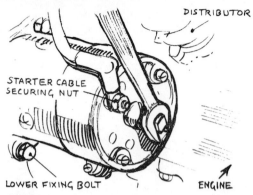

FIG 7:7 Using a spanner on the squared end of the starter motor shaft to free a jammed pinion

FIG 7:8 Loose or dirty battery connections may lead to starting difficulties

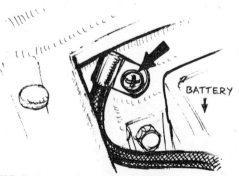

FIG 7:9 The battery earth cable is secured to the wing just in front of the battery. The connection must be clean and tight, with metal contacting metal. Check correct earthing system in Facts and Figures

(2) Starter motor just hums:

This is due to a faulty starter motor or to low current supply. Low current supply may be cured by attending to the battery and connections as covered in the preceding instructions. A faulty starter motor must be removed as instructed in the following sub-section. The most likely fault is a sticking pinion and this is easily cured.

(3) Starter motor turns engine slowly:

Again, this may be due to the same causes as those in the preceding sub-section. If a well-charged battery and good connections are no cure then the trouble lies either in bad contacts in the solenoid switch or a faulty starter motor. The solenoid switch will need renewal.

To remove the motor, disconnect the battery leads. Remove the cable shown in FIG 7:7 and the top bolt from the motor flange. With the front of the car jacked up and securely supported on blocks, remove the dirt shield and the lower bolt. Work the motor forward and lift it clear.

If the motor has been running without the drive engaging it may be due to dirt on the pinion assembly. Refer to FIG 7:10 and note the quick-thread on which the pinion slides. Wash the assembly in solvent such as petrol (in the open air, please) and when it is dry, check that the pinion moves freely. also check the heavy main spring and note that a very light spring returns the pinion, although it cannot be seen. Spring breakage makes the starter very noisy in operation (see sub-section 4). **Do not oil any part of the pinion assembly.**

If the motor drive still does not engage after this treatment, suspect a faulty motor or inadequate electrical supply. Cleaning the brushes and commutator is covered next.

(4) Starter motor is noisy:

The most likely cause is bearing wear or a faulty drive assembly. Continual jamming is a sign that the pinion teeth and those on the flywheel may be worn. Remove the motor as just described and check that the pinion springs are not broken (see FIG 7:10). If there is excessive clearance in the bearings when the shaft is rocked sideways, then the motor is due for renewal. The shaft should be free and make no scraping sounds when turned. It must also run true. Renewal of the motor is the only cure for a bent shaft.

Examine the pinion teeth. The forward faces are always rounded off to facilitate engagement, but if the teeth are obviously worn, renewal is indicated. Do not be surprised if new parts do not cure noise or jamming because the flywheel teeth may also be worn. This is a job for a service station.

On the subject of a bent shaft, remember that this is frequently due to operating the starter switch while the engine is running.

The best cure for a starter that shows signs of serious wear is to renew it on an exchange basis. Take your old starter to a dealer and collect a new or reconditioned one in its place. This is not expensive and it ensures that all wear and general deterioration is cured in one operation.

While the motor is on the bench it is a fairly easy matter to inspect the brushgear. Slacken the clamp screw and slide the coverband to one side (see **FIG 7:11**). If the interior is covered with dirt and copper dust this may be the reason why the motor does not run well. Brush out as much dirt as you can without using solvents. Check that the carbon brushes move freely by pulling on the flexible leads (see **FIG 7:12**). If the outer ends of the brushes are flush with the tops of the brass boxes in which they slide, they are due for renewal. This is a matter for a service station. A sticking brush may be lifted out by pulling the spring outwards with a wire hook. Rub the brush sides on a fine file to ease them. Make sure the brush returns to its original holder.

Clean the commutator with a petrol-moistened cloth (see **FIG 7:13**). Do not make the cloth too wet. Dry off thoroughly, and if necessary polish the copper segments with **very fine glasspaper (not emery-cloth)**. Wipe away all dust. Simply hold the glass-paper against the commutator and turn the shaft. This completes all the operations an amateur can do in the way of servicing.

B—Engine will not start—check ignition system:

FIG 7:14 gives the sequence for ignition checks. Although trouble in the fuel system may cause symptoms that are the same as those where the ignition is at fault, we propose to deal with ignition troubles first because they are the most likely reasons why the engine will not start. Check as follows:

(1) Checking wires and connections:

If the engine has given no sign of life, check that the thin wire to the side of the distributor is firmly connected (see **FIG 3:19** for location of ignition components). This connection is the one shown in **FIG 7:15**. Also check the leads going into the coil, and between the coil and distributor (see **FIG 7:16**). Try the starter with the ignition on and listen for sharp snapping sounds. If there is sparking between the high-tension cables and the body of the engine, the sparks will be audible and will show up clearly in the dark (see **FIG 7:34**). A temporary cure for such insulation breakdown is to use insulating tape or cellotape.

If there is a chance that the sparking plug leads have been wrongly connected, refer to **FIG 4:26**.

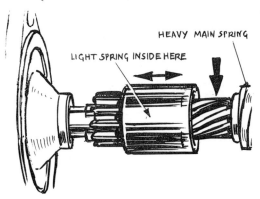

FIG 7:10 The starter motor pinion moves to and fro on a quick-thread. This thread must be clean and dry. Do not oil it

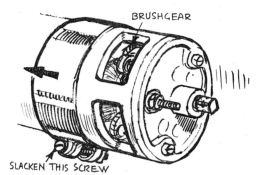

FIG 7:11 Slacken the clamping screw and slide back the cover to reveal the starter motor brushgear

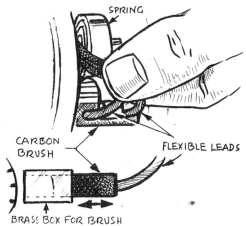

FIG 7:12 Pull on the brush leads to check that the carbon brushes move freely in their boxes

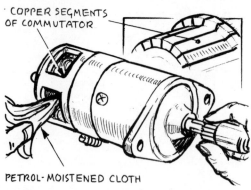

FIG 7:13 Use a small stick to press a fuel-moistened cloth onto the commutator whilst turning the shaft

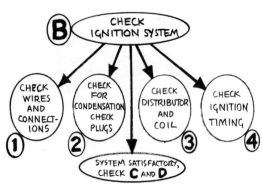

FIG 7:14 How to check the ignition system. The numbered sequence is covered in Section **B**

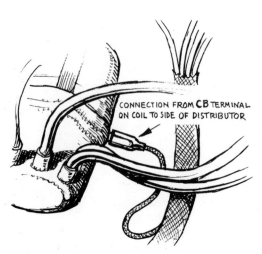

FIG 7:15 Check security of side connection to distributor (see above)

(2) Checking sparking plugs and checking for condensation:

A problem that arises when an engine is cold and stiff to turn is that the starter motor takes so much current that there is insufficient to produce fat sparks at the plugs. Any small loss of efficiency in the ignition department might then make starting very difficult.

The commonest cause of ignition trouble is condensation. This forms a conducting film that allows current to leak to earth. Dry off all moisture on leads and plug insulators with a warm cloth.

If the engine is still reluctant to start, remove the distributor cap, dry off the inside and check the carbon brush (see **Sections 4:12** and **4:13** in **Chapter 4**). Refit the cap and try again, being careful not to over-choke the engine or run the battery flat. Persistent trouble with condensation may be alleviated by using one of the spray-on inhibitors available at accessory shops.

If unsuccessful, check that current reaches the plugs. Unscrew one of them, refit the connector and hold the plug on its side on an adjacent clean metal part of the engine. Switch on the ignition. Press the starter button. There should be bright blue sparks at the plug electrodes (see **FIG 7:17**). This, however, does not guarantee sparks under pressure inside the cylinder, but it shows that the distributor and coil are functioning reasonably well.

You can avoid having to remove a plug by using one of the neon-tube devices sold in accessory shops. Turning the engine should then produce flashes from the neon tube. This proves that current reaches the plug, but the plug itself may still be faulty. Clean the plugs and check the gaps as in **Sections 4:11** and **4:12, Chapter 4**. Continued failure to start will then suggest tackling the fuel system.

If there is no spark the ignition system must be investigated as follows:

(3) Checking the distributor and coil:

The locations are shown in **FIG 3:19**. Remove the distributor cap as in **Section 4:9, Chapter 4**. Check the cap as in **Section 4:13, Chapter 4**.

Check the contact breaker points for gap as described in **Section 4:9, Chapter 4** and try to see whether the points are blackened or dirty. This may be due to oil or grease or to a faulty capacitor (condenser). Cleaning the points with a fuel-moistened cloth may effect a cure in the first case. Do not make the cloth too wet.

Turn the engine as described in **Section 4:9, Chapter 4** until the contact points are closed (see **FIG 4:28, Chapter 4**). Switch on the ignition and open the points with a screwdriver as in **FIG 7:18**. There should be a small blue spark across the points as they open, and a slight snapping sound will be heard. No spark indicates trouble with ignition circuit wiring, ignition switch or coil.

If the points do not open freely or have stuck open, apply **one** tiny drop of oil to the pivot and work the moving contact to and fro until it becomes free (see **FIG 5 : 6**).

To check the coil, first check that all connections are sound by peeling back the protecting cover (see **FIG 7 : 16**).

The terminals are marked CB and SW. The CB one is connected to the side of the distributor (see **FIG 7 : 15**). Disconnect the wire at both ends and connect a 12-volt test lamp across the vacant distributor and coil terminals. Switch on the ignition and turn the engine slowly or open and close the contact points by hand. The light should glow when the contact points close and go out when the points open. Try a new piece of connecting wire between the terminals if the lamp lights.

If the wire is not at fault, test the coil. Remove the CB wire from the coil (see **FIG 7 : 16**) and connect the test lamp between the coil tag and a good earth such as a clean metal part of the engine. Switch on the ignition. The lamp should light up. If it does not the coil is faulty. If the lamp does not light with the ignition switched on, remove test lamp clip from CB tag and connect it to the SW tag with the SW lead still in place. If lamp now lights up the coil winding has a break in it. If the lamp does not glow there is a fault in the ignition switch or the wiring between switch and coil. This will be a job for your service station.

To check the coil and circuit generally, remove the thick coil lead from the distributor cap. This is the central one that is held by a screw slightly offset from the carbon brush (see **FIG 7 : 19**). Remove the screw and pull out the lead. Note that the wire core can be seen at the end of the lead. Switch on the ignition. **Hold the lead with the fingers well away from the end** and bring it to within $\frac{1}{4}$ inch of a clean metal part of the engine (not the carburetter). Flick the closed contact points open. At each separation a fat blue spark should jump from the lead to the engine (see **FIG 7 : 20**). If there is no spark or the spark will only jump a tiny gap and is reddish in colour, the ignition system needs a complete overhaul. When fitting leads to the cap, use silicone grease on the open end to facilitate fitting and to make a watertight seal. Tighten the screw so that its point penetrates to the wire core. Do not use ordinary grease.

While the coil lead is detached from the distributor cap it is possible to check the rotor arm. Hold the coil lead about $\frac{1}{4}$ inch away from the brass part of the arm, switch on the ignition and operate the starter. If a spark jumps the gap the arm is defective. Look for cracks or carbon dust.

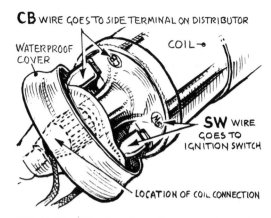

FIG 7 : 16 **Check all coil connections for security and good contact**

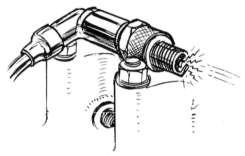

FIG 7 : 17 **Plug should spark when engine is turned and body of plug makes metallic contact with cylinder head**

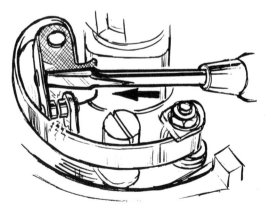

FIG 7 : 18 **There should be a tiny blue spark at the contact points when they are pushed apart with a small screwdriver. Ignition must be switched on**

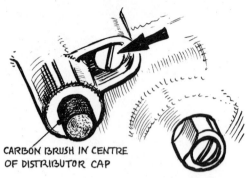

CARBON BRUSH IN CENTRE
OF DISTRIBUTOR CAP

FIG 7:19 Location of the screw that secures the coil lead into the distributor cap

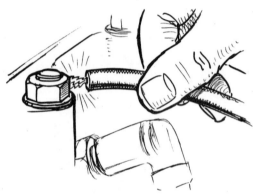

FIG 7:20 A healthy spark from the coil lead shows that the coil is satisfactory

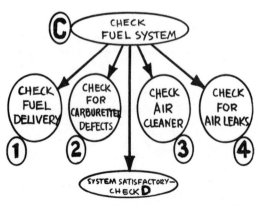

FIG 7:21 How to check the fuel system. The numbered sequence is covered in Section **C**

(4) Is the ignition timing at fault?

If the engine has been running well until now, it is unlikely that faulty ignition timing is the reason why it will not start. If, however, there are other symptoms like those described in the Section 'Engine runs badly' then the timing must be checked.

C—Engine will not start—check fuel system:

Refer to **FIG 7:21** for correct sequence of checking.

Having made the preliminary checks outlined in **Section 7:3**, there is an additional one that is quite simple and may avoid needless checking elsewhere. Switch on the ignition and tap the float chamber cover with a spanner (see **FIG 4:11**). This may loosen a sticking float needle and let the fuel pump operate. If the car has been standing some time after the attempt to start, get someone to switch on the ignition while you listen for the fuel pump to tick. The operation is covered in **Section 4:8, Chapter 4**.

If fuel is overflowing from the float chamber, try the cover-tapping trick first. If unsuccessful, switch off and check the float mechanism as in **Section 4:5, Chapter 4. Beware of fire!**

(1) Checking for fuel delivery:

At the carburetter end, check as described in **Section 4:8, Chapter 4.** If petrol is reaching the float chamber, check the float and needle valve as instructed for flooding in the earlier Section. A sticking needle valve will prevent the fuel pump from working.

If the engine stops on the road it is worth removing the fuel tank filler cap to check whether a partial vacuum has formed in the tank. This could happen if the vent pipe is blocked, and the vacuum would prevent fuel reaching the carburetter (see **FIG 7:38**). At the same time check for a blocked air vent hole in the filler cap.

(2) Carburetter defects:

Sticking piston:

May be the reason for difficult starting. Refer to **Section 4:6, Chapter 4** which gives instructions on the cure.

Choke control defective:

Pull the choke knob fully out and then return it. Place a finger under the carburetter jet and press upwards (see **FIG 4:6, Chapter 4**). If there is movement, the control system is faulty. Check the choke control cable (see **FIGS 4:23** in **Chapter 4** and **7:22**). Check the setting of the fast-idle screw (see **FIG 4:2, Chapter 4**).

Excessive fuel from choke control defects may be checked by removing a sparking plug. If the firing end is wet with petrol **(not oil),** remove all plugs and turn the engine by the starter to clear out excess fuel. Dry the plugs, refit them and try starting on less choke than usual (see **Section 7:3**). Plugs may be dried by heating over a gas ring or spirit stove.

Throttle mechanism defective:

With someone to operate the accelerator pedal, watch the lever on the side of the carburetter connected to the foremost of the two cables (see **FIG 7:22**). Check that it moves freely and returns to the stop. Check the adjustment of the stop (see **Section 4:4, Chapter 4**). If you cannot enlist a helper, pull upwards on the outer casing of the cable. This will also pull on the inner wire to operate the throttle. **Make sure the outer cable is fully returned into its socket after this check.**

(3) Air cleaner element choked:

If servicing has been neglected it is possible for a very dirty element to severely restrict the intake of air through the carburetter. Check this and fit a new element if necessary (see **Section 6:3, Chapter 6**). This is, however, likely to affect larger throttle openings rather than those required for starting, so leave checking this until last.

(4) Air leaks and contaminated fuel:

The carburetter may be correctly adjusted, but extra air may reduce the mixture strength if it enters the intake manifold at the joints shown in **FIG 7:23**. This could make starting from cold very difficult. Check all manifold nuts and those securing the carburetter flange. A faulty flange gasket could be renewed by a reasonably skilled amateur, but a new gasket for the manifolds is a job for a service station. A defective inlet manifold gasket often shows up by a whistling sound when the engine is running. Oil or water squirted round the joint will be sucked in at a defective place.

Another cause of difficulty in starting is the presence of water in the petrol. To check this, remove the float chamber cover (see **FIG 7:24** and **Section 4:5, Chapter 4**). Water globules will be seen in the bottom of the chamber and must be soaked out with non-fluffy rag or kitchen paper. If there are large accumulations of dirt or excessive quantities of water present, it is wise to have the whole fuel system of tank, pipes and pump checked by a garage.

D—Engine will not start—mechanical defects:

The sequence of defects is shown in **FIG 7:25**.
The quickest way to isolate mechanical defects is to have the engine vetted by a service station

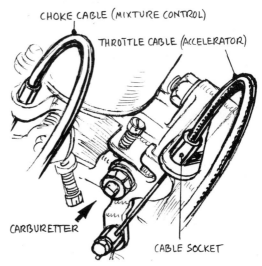

FIG 7:22 Choke and throttle cables must move freely and return fully

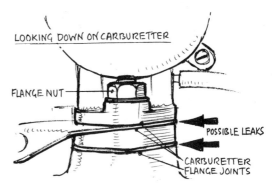

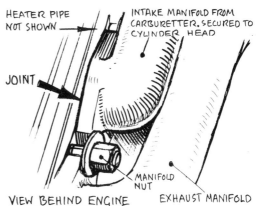

FIG 7:23 Air leaks may cause weak mixture. Check carburetter flange joints (top) and inlet manifold-to-cylinder head joints (bottom)

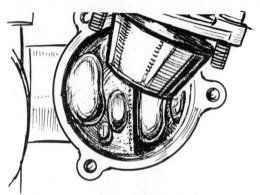

FIG 7:24 Remove the float chamber cover and check for globules of water

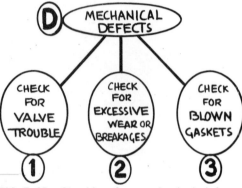

FIG 7:25 Checking for mechanical defects. The numbered sequence is covered in Section D

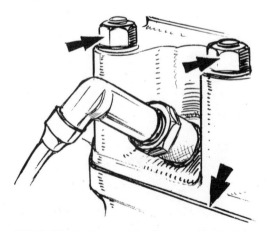

FIG 7:26 It is possible for a cylinder head gasket to be defective (lower arrow). Leakage may also be due to insufficiently tightened cylinder head nuts

equipped with diagnostic devices. Some of these checks take only a few minutes. For example, a compression test will quickly show up cylinder wear or valve defects.

(1) Valve trouble:

If the engine will not start and checks have revealed nothing apparently wrong in the three preceding systems, it is possible that there is a mechanical defect that is responsible. One of the most likely of these is valve trouble. If the engine tries to fire but spits back through the carburetter, the cause may be a valve that is remaining open, either because it is sticking, or through a broken spring, or it may be a valve or valves in poor condition.

Check by removing the rocker cover (see **Section 4:14, Chapter 4**). Turn the engine as described in **Section 4:9, Chapter 4**). Check the rocker clearances with each valve closed. If no clearance can be felt when using the rocker as a morse code key, adjust as in **Section 4:14, Chapter 4**. If the clearance is far in excess of the required clearance, check that the adjusting screw locknut is tight. If all is well at this point, do not adjust for the correct clearance, as this may be the sticking valve.

Tap downwards on the rocker tip to see whether the clearance increases or decreases. Take special care not to dislodge the pushrod at the adjusting end (see **FIG 4:48, Chapter 4**). Inject some penetrating oil onto the valve stem through the coils of the spring and try some more tapping. The valve may gradually become free and the clearance return to normal. This is, however, probably only a temporary cure and the trouble will almost certainly recur. The only permanent remedy is to have a new valve and/or guide fitted by the service station.

While the rocker cover is off, check that all the valve springs are sound. A broken spring may cause serious damage elsewhere and the engine ought not to be run until the trouble is rectified.

(2) Excessive wear or breakages:

The most likely defect that leads to starting difficulties will be wear or breakage of the valve mechanism. Most operations of detection and cure are a matter for a service station.

If the valves operate while the engine is turned, then the drive may be satisfactory.

While the engine is being turned, remove the distributor cap and check that the rotor arm is turning (see **FIG 4:27, Chapter 4**). If it does not move you have found the trouble. This is an extremely rare fault but very simple to check.

(3) Blown gaskets:

These are joint washers that must be leak-tight for an engine to start and run well. The carburetter

A defective cylinder head gasket as a cause of difficult starting is not so easy for the amateur to detect, but a compression test by a service station is one simple method. In any case, the engine may have been running badly for some time, there may be a curious whistling sound, or there may be a water leak into the engine (see **Section 4:29, Chapter 4**). The cure is relatively inexpensive, being the cost of a new head gasket and the labour of removing and refitting the cylinder head (see **FIG 7:26**). However, before jumping to conclusions it would be a good plan to let the service station check the cylinder head nuts for correct tightness, as slack nuts may be the cause of the trouble.

7:5 The engine runs badly

This Section deals with an engine that will start but then runs erratically, either misfiring, refusing to idle, stopping for no reason, or having no power (see **FIG 7:27**).

(1) Engine runs badly—misfires:

Try to differentiate between a regular and an erratic misfire. A regular misfire may be due to a defective sparking plug, a disconnected plug lead or to valve trouble in one cylinder. Refer to **Sections 4:11** and **4:12** in **Chapter 4** to cure the first two and to 'Mechanical defects, (D)' in the immediately preceding Section to check on the third.

An erratic misfire may be due to defective ignition, trouble in the fuel system or to some mechanical failure.

Check for ignition faults and the cures in **Sections 4:9, 4:11, 4:12** and **4:13** in **Chapter 4**, paying particular attention to sparking plugs, the contact breaker, the distributor cap and the plug leads. Ignition timing is not likely to be at fault.

Check for correct adjustment of the carburetter as described in **Sections 4:3, 4:4, 4:5, 4:6** and **4:7** in **Chapter 4**. Incorrect jet adjustment should be first on the checking list. Checking for air leaks and mechanical defects may also find the cause of the trouble (see the end of the preceding Section).

(2) Engine runs badly—will not idle:

This Section will also cover that fault when the engine stalls frequently for no apparent reason.

The most likely cause is faulty adjustment of the carburetter idling screw (see **Section 4:4, Chapter 4**). After this, check the adjustment of the mixture strength.

Follow this with the check for a flooding carburetter (see **Section 4:5, Chapter 4**) and for a sticking piston (see **Section 4:6, Chapter 4**).

Finally, read the preceding notes under 'Engine runs badly—misfires', as most of the symptoms will also apply to poor idling.

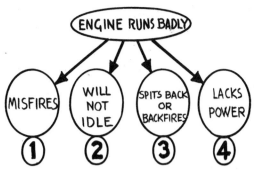

FIG 7:27 How to check when engine runs badly, using the numbered sequence in Section 7:5

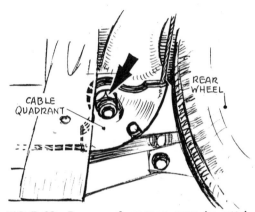

FIG 7:28 Poor performance may be attributable to rear brakes that stay partly on. The handbrake may not fully release if the cable quadrants are seized on their pivots. View is under rear subframe

FIG 7:29 Heavy oil consumption and black sludge inside the oil filler cap indicate a worn engine

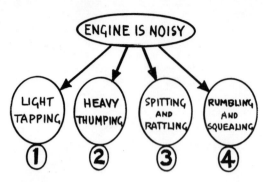

FIG 7:30 This numbered sequence is covered in Section 7:6

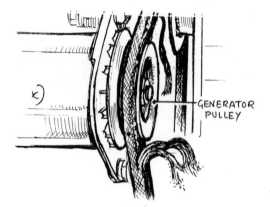

FIG 7:31 Check the fan belt for loose strands that may be striking against adjacent parts

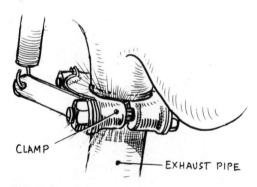

FIG 7:32 Exhaust gases may leak from the joint between the exhaust pipe and its manifold. The clamp will be found behind the engine, below the carburetter

Finally, read the preceding notes under 'Engine runs badly—misfires', as most of the symptoms will also apply to poor idling.

(3) Engine runs badly—spits back or backfires in the exhaust:

A snapping spit-back through the carburetter, probably accompanied by a smell of petrol under the bonnet from ejected mist out of the air cleaner, is generally due to weak mixture or weak ignition.

Check for mixture adjustment (see **Section 4:4, Chapter 4**). Check ignition system for defects leading to a weak spark (see **Sections 4:9, 4:12** and **4:13** in **Chapter 4**), starting with the sparking plugs.

Another cause of spitting-back is a sticking or faulty valve (see 'Valve trouble' in preceding **Section 7:4**). Also check for air leaks (see 'Air leaks and contaminated fuel').

Make sure that there is an element in the air cleaner (see **Section 6:3, Chapter 6**).

Backfiring in the exhaust system makes loud explosions and is due to unburnt mixture caused by weak ignition, weak mixture, or a sticking or defective valve. Check these as for 'spitting-back'.

(4) Engine runs badly—lacks power:

If the engine has had a long life without a major overhaul, or if the car has been bought secondhand, general wear and lack of tune may be the cause. The engine may also be in need of a decoke (decarbonizing), and this is often shown up by 'pinking' when accelerating hard from low speeds. 'Pinking' is a light tinkling sound from the engine which gradually fades as the engine speeds up. Understand, however, that this 'pinking' may also be due to inferior petrol or an ignition setting that is too far advanced.

If the engine still lacks power after a decoke it will be necessary to re-tune the engine as outlined in **Chapter 4**.

Poor performance from an engine may also be due to binding brakes. Ask your garage to examine the handbrake mechanism to the rear brakes for seizure of the cable quadrants (see **FIG 7:28**). The use of the wrong brake fluid may also lead to swollen rubber seals in the system and these may prevent the brakes from releasing after an application.

If the engine has been rebored, expect some falling-off in performance until it has been run-in.

It is possible that poor performance may be due to an engine with worn pistons, cylinders and valve gear. If your engine uses oil and the inside of the oil filler cap and rocker cover is thickly coated with black sludge, suspect wear as the reason for lack of power (see **FIG 7:29**). An inexpensive compression check by a garage will show up the faults, some of which may be due to faulty valves and seats.

A most unlikely cause of lost power may be incorrect valve timing. This might be the fault if an engine that previously ran well is down on power after a major overhaul or attention to the timing gear. If you have had a new timing chain fitted or a chain and sprockets, it is as well to raise the matter with the service station so that the timing can be checked.

7 : 6 The engine is noisy (see FIG 7 : 30) :

The locating of unusual sounds can be quite baffling and it is advisable to seek expert advice if the sounds have become noticeable after a long run at high speeds, or if they are accompanied by a sudden rise in oil consumption, a fall in performance or by overheating. Do not run the engine if the noise is accompanied by the continued glow of the oil pressure warning light.

If the sound is heard while motoring, try coasting along in neutral. If it then persists it is unlikely to be something to do with the engine. If it rises and falls in neutral, in response to accelerator movement, it is probably an engine fault.

(1) Light tapping sounds :

The commonest cause will be excessive valve clearances (see **Section 4 : 14, Chapter 4**). If these are correct, run the engine fast and then shut off suddenly. If the clicking is slow and gradually disappears it may be due to a sticking valve. This problem is discussed in **D** in **Section 7 : 4**. A sticking valve will also cause misfiring. Do not confuse 'tapping' with 'pinking' as discussed in the preceding Section. 'Pinking' will disappear when the engine is idling. A light slapping sound that disappears when the engine is hot is most likely to be due to worn pistons and cylinders. Suspect this if the engine uses oil. Reboring or a replacement engine is the best cure.

One other cause may be a loose strand of fan belt that is slapping against some part of the engine or cowling. While checking the belt, check the security of the generator pulley (see **FIG 7 : 31**).

(2) Heavy thumping sounds :

Having checked that these are confined to the engine, try to remember what happens on the road. If the sounds die out when the engine is pulling, but reappear when the accelerator pedal is eased back, the trouble may be failure of one or more big-ends. Run the engine in neutral and try to repeat the sounds. Pull off and replace each sparking plug lead in turn. Any reduction in the sound at a particular

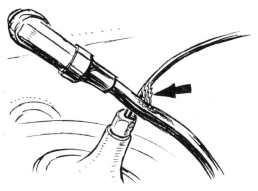

FIG 7 : 33 Snapping sounds may be due to sparking from a faulty high-tension lead to an adjacent metal earth

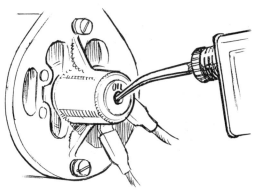

FIG 7 : 34 A few drops of oil on the generator rear bearing may cure a squealing noise.

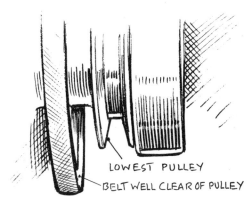

LOWEST PULLEY
BELT WELL CLEAR OF PULLEY

FIG 7 : 35 It is possible to run the engine without turning the generator or the fan and water pump. Remove the belt from the pulleys and keep the lowest part of belt clear of the engine pulley

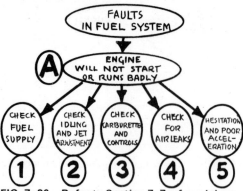

FIG 7:36 Refer to Section 7:7 for advice on fuel faults that lead to engine trouble

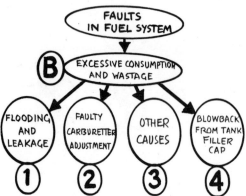

FIG 7:37 The second part of Section 7:7 deals with fuel faults leading to excessive consumption

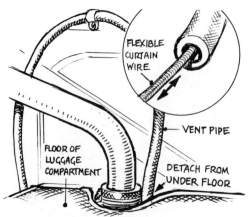

FIG 7:38 Blowback when filling with petrol may be due to a blocked vent pipe. Detach the pipe and pass a flexible wire through it (see inset)

cylinder will locate the fault. **Do not continue to run the engine.** A complete engine overhaul will be necessary. Particularly heavy thumping sounds that accompany starting up, accelerating and pulling under load and are definitely confined to the engine, may be due to main bearing wear or a loose flywheel. Repeat the preceding test with the disconnected sparking plugs. A very short run under light loading is permissible to reach a service station. The engine will need removing from the car for attention.

(3) Spitting and rattling sounds:

A frequent cause of a spitting sound is a faulty exhaust pipe connection to the manifold behind the engine (see **FIG 7:32**). Try tightening the clamp bolts, **but do not overdo this or the clamp may be distorted.** It may be necessary to renew the exhaust system.

Other spitting sounds may be traceable to leaking joint gaskets, particularly at the manifolds behind the engine (see **FIG 7:23**) and round the cylinder head joint (see **FIG 7:26**). Sometimes, leaking gases may be felt by the bare hand. Such leaks will always cause uneven running unless they are in the exhaust system. Renewal of the gaskets is comparatively inexpensive.

Closely related to spitting sounds are the snapping sounds from shortcircuits in the sparking plug wiring (see **Section 4:13** in **Chapter 4** and **FIG 7:33**).

Rattles can be annoying and elusive. Let the engine idle and pull off a plug lead connector to induce misfiring. This may accentuate the rattle. Suspect the exhaust pipe connection behind the engine, and also check the fan and cowling. **Do not do this with the engine running.** Make sure the generator and coil mountings are secure (see **FIG 4:52, Chapter 4**). Check the air cleaner fixings.

On a well-worn engine the rattle may be due to a worn timing chain. This is housed below the fan and water pump. The rattle will probably be loudest when the engine is idling and a plug lead has been removed to induce misfiring and rough running. The only cure is renewal of the worn parts.

(4) Rumbling and squealing:

Steady rumbling from the engine may be due to bearing wear, either in the water pump or at the drive end of the generator. Up and down play will be a sure sign of bearing wear and renewal on an exchange basis is the best cure. A stethoscope is a ready means of locating the fault or a hand placed in the suspected area may feel the source of the rumbling, **but please make sure the fingers are clear of the fan and belt.** Squealing is almost certain to be coming from the end of the generator opposite to the pulley. Try introducing two or three drops of oil (see **FIG 7:34**). If this does not cure the trouble suspect the generator brush gear. This must be checked by a service station.

If the fan belt is removed from the pulleys (see **Section 4:15, Chapter 4**) and the rumbling or squealing vanishes with the engine running, the water pump or generator is definitely at fault. It is not necessary to remove the belt completely, providing it is tied back out of the way of the lowest pulley (see **FIG 7:35**). Do not run the engine too long without the water pump.

It is just possible that a squeak may emanate from the distributor. This will be due to an unlubricated cam. Apply a touch of grease as shown in **FIG 5:6**.

7:7 Troubleshooting the fuel system

A—Engine will not start or runs badly:

The series of likely causes are given in **FIG 7:36**. It will be found that most of the problems have already been covered in **C** in **Section 7:4** where it will be seen that the fuel system may not necessarily be the culprit. Faulty ignition or mechanical defects may give the same symptoms.

(1) Checking fuel supply:

Refer to **Section 7:3** and then to **C** in **Section 7:4**. Matters connected with the operation of the electric fuel pump are covered in **Section 4:8, Chapter 4**.

(2) Checking idling and jet adjustments:

Refer to **Section 7:4** to solve those problems likely to be connected with incorrect adjustment of the carburetter (also see **Section 4:4, Chapter 4**).

(3) Checking for defective carburetter or controls:

The effects and cures of faults in these items are covered in **Section 7:4**.

(4) Checking for air leaks:

See **C** in **Section 7:4**, which deals with the effects and cures of air leaks.

(5) Hesitation or poor acceleration:

Check for a sticking piston (see **Section 4:6, Chapter 4**). Check fuel level in float chamber (see **Section 4:5, Chapter 4**) and check that the damper is filled with the correct grade of oil to the required level (see **Section 5:3, Chapter 5**). A check should be made for air leaks (see preceding sub-section).

B—Fuel consumption is excessive:

Refer to **FIG 7:37**.

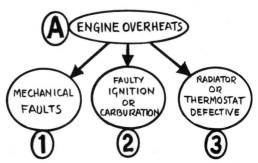

FIG 7:39 Faults in the cooling system leading to an overheated engine are covered in Section 7:9

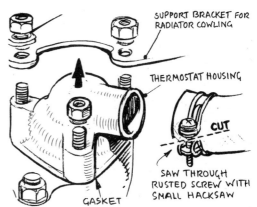

FIG 7:40 Access to the thermostat is gained by removing three nuts and lifting off the housing

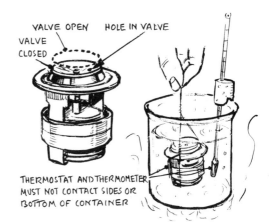

FIG 7:41 Check operation of thermostat valve by immersing in hot water. Hole in valve must by kept clear of deposits

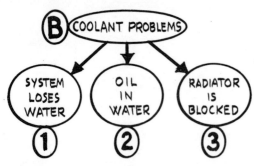

FIG 7:42 The second part of Section 7:9 covers faults connected with the coolant

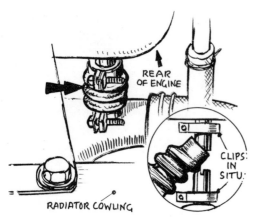

FIG 7:43 Location of bypass hose behind engine. It is easier to fit the clips before manipulating the new hose into place (see inset)

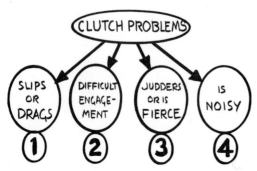

FIG 7:44 This sequence of clutch problems is covered in Section 7:10

(1) Check for flooding and leakage:

Check float chamber for flooding (see **Section 4:5, Chapter 4**). Check system for leaking pipes and connections.

(2) Faulty carburetter adjustments:

The effect and cure for these is covered in **Section 7:4**.

(3) Heavy consumption due to other causes:

These include faulty ignition or mechanical defects in the engine. Another reason may be bad driving habits (see **Section 3:18, Chapter 3**) or binding brakes (see **Section 7:5**).

(4) Blowback from the tank filler:

If petrol blows back from the pipe when filling-up it may be due to a blockage in the tank vent pipe. Release the top end of the pipe and push down a length of flexible wire (see **FIG 7:38**). The pipe ends below the car body and may be blocked with road dirt. Reconnect the pipe afterwards.

7:8 Troubleshooting the ignition system

If the engine will not start, or runs badly, give high priority to an investigation of the ignition system. Without trying to confuse you we must, however, point out that the same symptoms may be due to fuel or mechanical failure!

For the effect of ignition troubles on the engine, see B in **Section 7:4**. Checking and adjustment of the ignition system is fully covered in **Sections 4:9 to 4:13 in Chapter 4**.

7:9 Troubleshooting the cooling system

A—Engine overheats:

The probable causes are indicated in **FIG 7:39**. **Before discussing these we must emphasise the need for extreme caution when releasing the radiator or expansion tank caps when the system is hot, as scalding by steam is likely** (see **FIG 3:9, Chapter 3**).

(1) Engine overheats—mechanical faults:

Belt may be broken. Check for a slipping belt. Renew belt if oily. Tighten belt if loose (see **Section 4:15, Chapter 4**). Check all hoses for collapse that may be restricting coolant circulation. The engine may run hotter for a time after a rebore.

(2) Engine overheats—faulty ignition or carburation:

A weak spark or ignition timing that is incorrect may be the cause. Check the timing as advised in **Section 4:10, Chapter 4**. Weak mixture from the carburetter may also be the reason. Check the jet adjustment as in **Section 4:4, Chapter 4.** Another cause may be air leaks (see **C** in **Section 7:4**).

(3) Engine overheats—radiator or thermostat defective:

Radiator problems are covered in **Section B.**

The thermostat is a temperature-operated valve at the water outlet from the cylinder head (see **FIG 7:40**). The valve is closed when starting from cold, to give a rapid warm-up. It opens when hot to let the coolant reach the top of the radiator.

If the valve fails to open the coolant will boil. Conversely, if it does not close when cold, the engine will take a long time to warm-up.

Removing and checking the thermostat is a simple matter.

Drain the radiator and remove the top hose from the thermostat housing (see illustration). Remove the cowling support bracket and the third nut and tap the cover gently to release it. Lift it off the studs and prise out the thermostat. If this is obviously in a bad state renew it.

To check the thermostat, suspend it in water as shown in **FIG 7:41** without allowing it to touch the sides or the bottom of the container together with a thermometer. Gently heat the water and observe the operation of the thermostat valve. It should start to open at 180°F (82°C) and if it fails to open within a few degrees of this figure, the thermostat must be renewed as neither repair nor adjustment are possible. Check that the hole in the valve is clear.

When refitting a thermostat (valve upwards) fit a new gasket.

B—Coolant problems:

Refer to **FIG 7:42**.

(1) System loses water:

If, at the same time, the engine oil level **rises,** see **Section 4:29, Chapter 4** under 'Loss of water (coolant)'. The fault is serious and must have immediate attention.

The other possibility is leakage. This will show up as damp patches on the floor. Usually it is due to defective hoses. If they are cracked and flabby, renew them. If the screws of the clips have rusted solid, saw through them and fit new clips.

One hose that may be missed is the bypass hose behind the engine at the radiator end (see **FIG 7:43**). It is possible to fit a new hose without lifting the cylinder head but it is a tricky job and needs a great deal of patience. It is essential to fit the clips over the metal tubes first and then draw them back over the fitted hose.

If water comes from the underside of the water pump it is getting past the seal in the pump. As new pumps can be obtained on an exchange basis, it is a

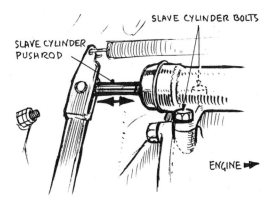

FIG 7:45 Pushrod and operating lever should move freely when the clutch pedal is depressed

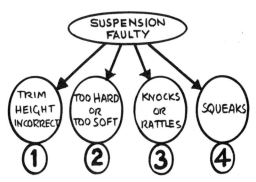

FIG 7:46 See Section 7:12 for coverage of suspension problems

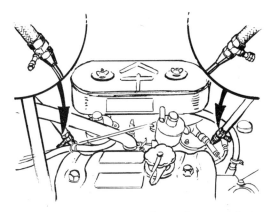

FIG 7:47 These are the valves used to pressurize the suspension system. Never interfere with them

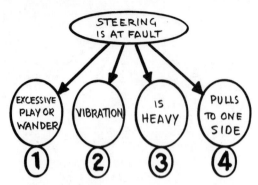

FIG 7:48 This sequence of steering problems is discussed in Section 7:13

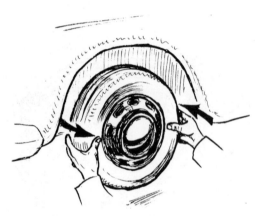

FIG 7:49 Move jacked-up wheel gently in and out to check for free play in the steering mechanism

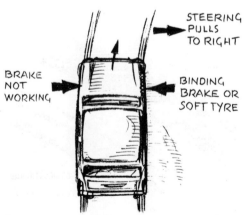

FIG 7:50 How defective brakes or a soft tyre will upset the steering, causing a pull to one side

(2) There is oil in the water:

Refer to **Section 4:29** which covers this problem and its cure.

(3) The radiator is blocked:

This is an unlikely cause of overheating unless the car is quite old. The simplest method of clearing deposits is to buy a proprietary radiator cleaning kit and follow the instructions.

7:10 Clutch problems

FIG 7:44 shows the sequence of problems.

(1) Clutch slips or drags:

If the clutch is fully engaged (pedal right back) with the gearlever in 'TOP' and engine speed can be increased without a corresponding increase in road speed, the clutch is slipping. First check the clearance of the operating lever (see **Section 4:19, Chapter 4**). If correct, get someone to operate the clutch pedal while you watch the pushrod at the top (see **FIG 7:45**). If it seems quite free to move, the fault may be in the master cylinder or there may be oil on the clutch. Both these are matters for a service station.

Clutch drag means noisy gear engagement and a tendency for the car to move off even though the pedal is fully depressed. Excessive clearance may be the cause (see **Section 4:19, Chapter 4**). If not, bleed the hydraulic system (see **Section 4:20, Chapter 4**). Check the system for leaks. Other causes may be defects in the operating cylinders or in the clutch itself and these are both jobs for a service station. Before becoming too involved, check that the carpets are not preventing the pedal from being fully depressed.

(2) Clutch engagement is difficult:

If the clutch will not engage, check the clearance as in **Section 4:19, Chapter 4**. If the clutch will not disengage, check the carpets as in the preceding instructions. In fact, the symptoms are the same as those for clutch drag and the cures will be the same.

(3) Clutch judders or is fierce:

If takeoff at low speeds and engine revolutions is not smooth (the effect is particularly noticeable in 'reverse') the trouble may be oil on the clutch plate or to some other clutch defect. First, let your garage check all the engine and exhaust pipe mountings and have softened ones renewed. Check the slave cylinder bolts for security (see **FIG 7:45**).

If the juddering persists there is nothing for it but to have the clutch inspected.

(4) Clutch is noisy:

This is always an internal fault and dismantling is a service station job.

7:11 Transmission troubles

There is nothing a normal owner can do about any of the troubles likely to affect the transmission, either manual or automatic. Noise must be associated with wear or loose fixings. Jumping out of gear or difficult gear engagement are problems needing the experts. If there is no drive whatever, suspect the clutch first. If it is not the clutch then there must be a fault in the gearbox or drive shafts. In every case, the unfortunate owner must seek help from an authorised dealer.

7:12 Suspension problems

The sequence of troubles is shown in **FIG 7:46.**

(1) Suspension trim height incorrect:

This shows up if the car is lop-sided or seems to be higher or lower than it should be. There is an easy check for this (see **Section 6:7, Chapter 6**). The cure is to have the system repressurized by a dealer. **Never interfere with the valves used to pressurize the system** (see **FIG 7:47**).

(2) Suspension is too hard or too soft:

If too hard, try pressing up and down on the front or rear bumpers to 'bounce' the car. If the suspension unit at one or more of the wheels seems excessively resistant to movement, get it checked for seizure or a faulty unit. If all the units work well, have the pressure checked because it will be too high.

If too soft, an increase in pressure will help. Alternatively, softness at one wheel may be due to a fault in that unit.

(3) Suspension knocks or rattles:

These may be traceable by the method shown in **FIG 4:102, Chapter 4.** Jack up the car and check all suspension fixings for security. Shake each wheel vigourously to see whether there is excessive play anywhere, taking care, however, not to shake the car off the jack. If the knocking comes from the front end it may not be the suspension system but the drive shaft joints that are at fault. Your service station will need to check for this (see **FIG 4:101, Chapter 4**).

(4) Suspension squeaks:

'Bounce' the car to check whether the squeak is at the front or the rear. If at the front, check the lubrication of the swivel hubs (see **Section 5:3 (8), Chapter 5**). The squeak may be coming from the rubber bushes shown in **FIG 4:102, Chapter 4** or from those at the inner ends of the lower suspension

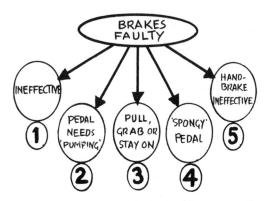

FIG 7:51 Trouble with the braking system is covered by the numbered sequence in Section 7:14

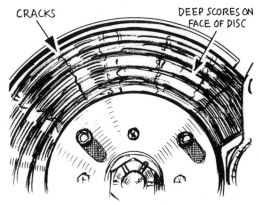

FIG 7:52 Remove the front wheels and check the brake discs for cracks and deep scoring. These defects may cause grabbing or pulling to one side

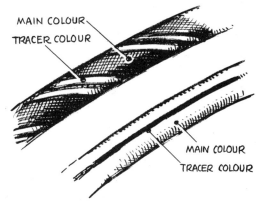

FIG 7:53 Wires with two-colour coding have a main colour and a thin tracer colour

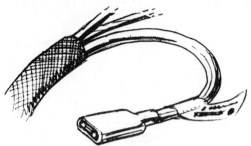

FIG 7:54 Identify detached wiring so that it can be reconnected correctly

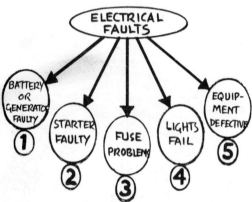

FIG 7:55 Work through the numbered sequence in Section 7:15 to cure electrical faults

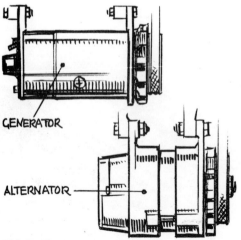

FIG 7:56 How to tell whether your car is fitted with a generator or an alternator

arms. Lubricate with rubber grease or brake fluid. Failure to cure the squeaks in this way calls for expert investigation as other points may be the cause, and the cure is then not so easy.

7:13 Troubleshooting the steering system

The checking sequence is given in **FIG 7:48**.

(1) Steering has excessive play or car wanders:

Check the play as in **Section 6:7, Chapter 6. Section 4:28, Chapter 4** covers the likely causes for play and wander. Also check for tyre defects as covered in **Section 4:27, Chapter 4**.

Jack up the front wheels and move each wheel **gently** in and out as shown in **FIG 7:49. Do not reverse the movement violently or serious damage to the steering gear may result.** Watch the outer ball joints (see **FIG 6:6, Chapter 6**). Check for excessive movement in the swivel hub joints (see **FIG 5:2, Chapter 5**). If the tie-rods respond instantly to wheel movement (see **FIG 6:5, Chapter 6**), suspect free-play in the steering gearbox but first check that the assembly is firmly secured by the U-bolts shown in the illustration. Renewal of the ball joints is relatively inexpensive. Always suspect wear as the cause of free-play if rubber boots or bellows are damaged (see **Section 6:6, Chapter 6**).

Finally, check the car trim as instructed in **Section 6:7, Chapter 6**, as this may cause wander if incorrect.

(2) Steering vibrates:

Check all the points covered in 'Steering play' in **Section 4:28, Chapter 4**. The most likely cause is out-of-balance or buckled wheels. If this is not so, check for free-play as in the preceding sub-section. A car that has had accident damage to the front end must have all the steering angles accurately checked by a service station.

(3) Steering is heavy:

See the preceding notes on accident damage. Make sure that the front tyre pressures are not habitually too low. Check the lubrication of the swivel hubs (see **FIG 5:2, Chapter 5**).

Check the steering gear for faulty rubber boots or bellows and make sure the steering rack is firmly secured (see preceding **sub-section 1**).

If the fault cannot be isolated, suspect the steering gearbox or its lubrication.

(4) Steering pulls to one side:

First check the tyre pressures, followed by the trim heights (see **Section 6:7, Chapter 6**). Wheel alignment may be at fault, particularly after an accident, so have the subframe mountings and steering angles checked by specialists. Make sure the pull is not due to a binding brake (see **FIG 7:50**). **Section 4:16, Chapter 4** gives instructions on inspecting the front brakes, but if the pistons cannot be pressed back after the pads are removed, then suspect seizure as the cause.

A front brake that is binding will affect the steering far more than one at the rear. The disc will become very hot.

Pulling may only be noticed whilst braking. This is almost certainly due to a defective front brake. Check the one on the side opposite to the pull for defective pads or oil on the disc (see **Section 4:16, Chapter 4**).

7:14 Trouble with the brakes

FIG 7:51 gives a checking sequence. With most braking problems it is essential to be sure that the front pads and rear linings are of the correct grade and have equal wear.

(1) Brakes ineffective:

If the brakes seem feeble and need excessive pressure on the pedal, check the rear brake adjustment (see **Section 4:17, Chapter 4**). Check the front brake pads (see **Section 4:16, Chapter 4**). If necessary, remove the pads and check that the pistons are free to move. There must be no oil or grease on the discs.

If these investigations reveal nothing untoward, have the rear brake drums removed for a check of the linings and operating mechanism.

(2) Brake pedal needs 'pumping':

The pedal will have excessive travel, which will be taken up by operating it several times. Check that there is plenty of fluid in the master cylinder reservoir (see **Section 5:3 (5), Chapter 5**). Try adjusting the rear brakes first (see **Section 4:17, Chapter 4**). If this does not cure the trouble, bleed the system (see **Section 4:18, Chapter 4**). Check for leaks (see **Sections 4:18 and 4:28, Chapter 4**).

If there is still no cure, there is probably some defect in the master cylinder or in the wheel cylinders. **Be very suspicious if there is a need for constant topping-up of brake fluid.** Let your garage give the system a thorough check.

(3) Brakes pull to one side, grab, or stay on:

Check that tyres are evenly inflated. Check rear brake adjustment and condition of front pads (see **Sections 4:16 and 4:17, Chapter 4**). Feeling the temperature of rear drums and front discs will show up the cool brakes that are ineffective or those that are pulling and becoming much hotter.

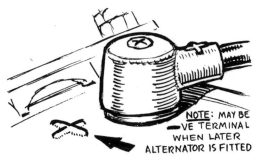

FIG 7:57 **Make sure the battery is connected with the positive (+) terminal lead joined to a clean metal earthing point on the body (see also FIG 7:9). This may be the negative (—) terminal on later cars fitted with an alternator (see Facts and Figures)**

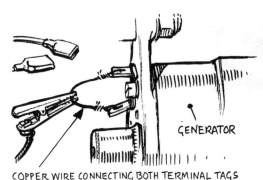

FIG 7:58 **Connecting a test lamp to check the output from the generator**

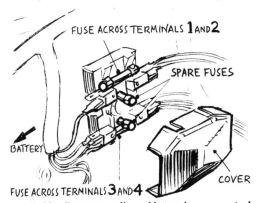

FIG 7:59 **Fuses are clipped into a box mounted on the righthand wing valance, under the bonnet. Note the push-on cover and the two spare fuses**

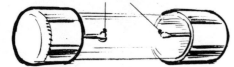

MELTED ENDS OF FUSE WIRE

FIG 7:60 How you will recognize a burnt-out fuse

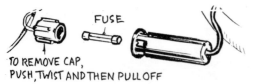

FUSE

TO REMOVE CAP, PUSH, TWIST AND THEN PULL OFF

FIG 7:61 The separate fuse for side and tail lamps

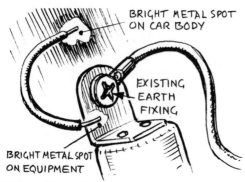

BRIGHT METAL SPOT ON CAR BODY

EXISTING EARTH FIXING

BRIGHT METAL SPOT ON EQUIPMENT

FIG 7:62 Check for efficient earthing by trying a substitute earth wire connected to clean metallic surfaces

PANEL FIXINGS

FIG 7:63 On de-luxe models, the facia panel must be removed to gain access to the warning light bulbs

Remove the front wheels and check the discs (see FIG 7:52). The surface must be only lightly scored and must not be cracked or running out of true. Have the rear drums removed for a similar check of the shoes and the braking surfaces.

Brakes that grab suddenly, even on light pedal application may have distorted discs or drums. Have these checked. Also check for loose rear backplates. These are the plates that are shown in FIG 4:63, Chapter 4.

Brakes that will not come off may have the rear brakes too closely adjusted (see Section 4:17, Chapter 4). Rear brakes often do not release because the cable quadrants have seized on their pivots (see FIG 7:28). This is a job for a service station. Go for a short run without using the brakes and check the temperatures of the drums. A drum that is hot even though the adjustment is correct and the cable quadrant quite free has an internal defect.

Front brake disc temperatures may also be checked in the same way. Failure of front brakes to release will probably be due to seized operating pistons and these need the attention of your garage.

(4) Brake pedal is 'spongy':

The most likely cause is air in the system. Check the fluid in the master cylinder reservoir (see Section 5:3 (5), Chapter 5) and then bleed the brakes as instructed in Section 4:18, Chapter 4.

(5) The handbrake is ineffective:

Check rear brake adjustment (see Section 4:17, Chapter 4). Have rear brake drums removed for a check of the friction linings. Ask the garage to check that the wheel cylinders are free to slide in the backplates. With good linings and correct adjustment the handbrake should work well if the cable quadrants are not seized (see FIG 7:28).

7:15 Troubleshooting the electrical system

The elusive electrical fault is a trial to most car owners, particularly when it involves short circuits or wiring failure. A simple test lamp or a 12-volt meter with prods will prove invaluable. The clue to colour-coding of the wires is given in FIG 7:53. Faulty equipment is a different matter. Major items such as the generator and the starter motor are readily available on an exchange basis. If your equipment shows defects due to age it is wise to renew it by trading it in.

If you detach wires at any time, mark or identify each wire and connection for correct refitting (see FIG 7:54).

A simple sketch is also a good idea. Wipe the wires free from dirt so that you can see the colour coding.

Do not disconnect equipment or leave wires hanging loose without first disconnecting the battery, or there may be trouble with shorting.

The push-on connectors are sometimes clipped on with special tools. If you are skilled enough and wish to renew wiring, it is possible to solder a new cable to an old connector.

Note that all references to 'earthing' mean that the electrical circuit to a unit is completed through its wiring and the steelwork of the body and mountings. The battery is also earthed (see **FIG 7:9**), and that is how current reaches the various pieces of equipment. The body is, in effect, the second wire.

The most likely electrical faults are shown in **FIG 7:55,** and the following sections will tell you how to deal with them.

(1) Electrical trouble—battery or generator at fault:

Battery faulty:

If the battery needs frequent topping-up, look for a cracked casing. Leaking acid will cause severe corrosion of surrounding metalwork but this may occur even with a sound casing. If the battery seems to be in good condition, get your dealer to check the generator output for a charging rate that is too high.

If the battery will not hold a charge or is quite dead, suspect a defective battery if the car is used regularly in daylight and topping-up has not been neglected. Remember, too, that if the ignition is left switched on all night, the drain on the battery may discharge it.

Section 5:4 (12), Chapter 5 tells you how to check a battery. Note that leaving a battery in a discharged state may eventually lead to complete failure.

Have a discharged battery recharged. If it stays charged, it may have been run-down by excessive night driving and prolonged attempts at starting. If it becomes discharged again without heavy demands being made on it, then either the battery or the generating system is at fault. If a new battery has just been fitted, make sure it is correctly connected (see **FIG 7:57**).

If you have an alternator like that shown in FIG 7:56, do not run the engine with the battery or any of the wiring disconnected.

On most models the positive (+) terminal of the battery is earthed (connected to the car body). Cars with the latest type of alternator (16ACR) have the negative (—) terminal earthed (see **FIG 7:57** and **Facts and Figures**).

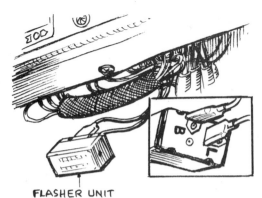

FLASHER UNIT

FIG 7:64 The later type of flasher unit is located behind the facia panel. Note the two terminal tags L and B

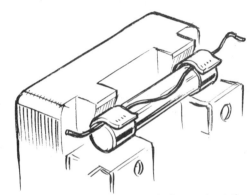

FIG 7:65 Before adjusting the horn, short the fuse connecting terminals 1 and 2 with a piece of wire

DO NOT DISTURB THIS SCREW

ADJUSTING SCREW

FIG 7:66 Carrying out adjustment to the horn. Note that central screw must not be disturbed

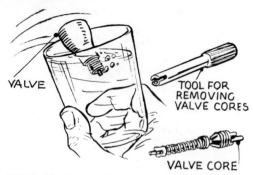

FIG 7:67 Immersing tyre valve in water to test for leaks (left). A valve core, and removing or inserting tool (right)

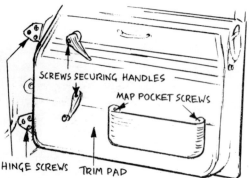

FIG 7:68 Details of door fixings. Remove handles and map pocket to prise off trim pad

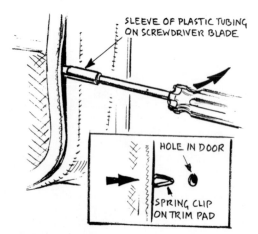

FIG 7:69 Prising away the door trim pad. Pad is refitted by pressing the spring clips into place with a light blow

Generator or alternator faulty:

Output from the generator or alternator may be low due to a slipping belt. The belt may be loose or oily. Tightening or renewal is covered in **Section 4:15, Chapter 4.**

If a good battery remains in a low state of charge, have the generator system checked, particularly if the red ignition warning light does not go out at fast idling engine speeds. If the light stays on all the time the first check must be for a broken belt (see **Section 4:15, Chapter 4**).

If you have an alternator instead of a generator (compare them in **FIG 7:56**) make sure all connections are tight and note the warning just given.

Apparent failure of a generator (**not an alternator**) may be checked as follows:

Note how the wires are connected and then pull them off the tags on the generator (see **FIG 7:58**).

Connect the tags with copper wire. Clip one lead of a 12-volt test lamp to the wire and press the other lead onto a clean metal part of the generator body. **The bulb should light at moderate engine speeds. Racing the engine will burn out the bulb.**

If you cannot obtain full brightness of the lamp, suspect the generator. It may be repairable or it may need renewal. If you are happy with spanners it is fairly simple to detach the wires and the ignition coil bracket and remove the generator (see **FIGS 4:52** in **Chapter 4** and **5:11** in **Chapter 5**). Fit the new unit, connect the wires properly and adjust the belt.

(2) Electrical trouble—starter faulty:

All the tests and cures for a faulty starter are covered in **Section 7:4 (A).**

(3) Electrical trouble—fuse problems:

The fuses are on the righthand wing valance (see **FIG 7:59**). The cover is a push-on fit. The terminal tags are marked 1, 2, 3 and 4. The fuse across terminals 1 and 2 protects equipment that works without the ignition switched on, namely the horn and the interior lights. The fuse across 3 and 4 protects equipment operating with the ignition switched on. This includes the flashers, wiper, heater, fuel gauge and stop lights. **Use 35-amp fuses as replacements. Never fit a fuse with a higher rating and never use wire, nails or silver paper as a substitute.**

There is a separate fuse for the side and tail lamps. This is fitted in a tubular housing located in various places. It may be under the battery or under the facia. On 1100/1300 de luxe models it is under the righthand side of the parcel shelf. **FIG 7:61** shows how the fuse is removed by pushing the tubes together, en giving them a twist. This fuse is also rated at 5-amp.

If some equipment fails to operate, check the ses. The ends of the broken fuse wire will be early seen through the glass (see **FIG 7:60**). ut all switches off and fit a new fuse (there are two ares in the fuse box). If the fuse blows again, neck all wiring and units between the battery and e fuse. Pay particular attention to wiring exposed damp and dirt. If the fuse blows with the switches n, there is a fault between the fuse and the earth iring. If no fault can be found ask your dealer to rry out a comprehensive check.

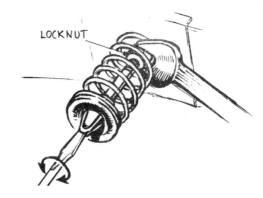

FIG 7:70 To adjust the bonnet catch, slacken the locknut and turn the bolt as required

) Electrical trouble—lights fail:

Bulbs that are dim even though the battery is well-narged may be discoloured with age or they may ave poor connections. Push and pull on the nnectors to check for good contact.

To check earth connections to the body, connect wire between a clean part of the existing fixing nd a bright spot on the body (see **FIG 7:62**). heck the battery terminals as in **A** in **Section 7:4**.

If a bulb fails, check it across a battery. If it lights p, check the holder contacts and wiring con-ections. Check the switch if possible. Do not prod ound with a screwdriver or you may blow a fuse. se a slip of wood instead.

If all seems well, suspect the wiring. You will be ble to bypass a faulty wire with a length of similar ire connected to the supply and the bulbholder. If the ulb lights, cut the old wire short at the loom (the nclosure round a pack of wires) and insulate the nds with tape. Solder the ends of the new wire to e clips to make a permanent job.

FIG 7:71 The Autobook Workshop Manual for all 1100/1300 models gives comprehensive instructions for complete overhaul (see Section 7:19)

) Electrical faults—equipment is defective:

ashers (direction indicators) faulty:

Rapid flashing is generally due to a blown flasher ulb. Renew it as described in **Section 4:22, hapter 4.** Slow flashing may be due to a faulty asher unit or to bulbs of the wrong type.

If one flasher bulb will not light and it is known to e good, check the wiring and contacts.

Flashers that do not work may indicate a blown se. Check as suggested in the earlier Section on ses. There may be a fault in the wiring or the unit. emember to switch on the ignition.

Warning lights give some clues to faulty operation. Vhen two warning lights are fitted, both will go out the flasher unit is faulty. If one flasher bulb fails, the arning light on that side will also go out. Before necking the unit, make sure that the warning light ulb(s) is not burned out. Unscrew the green plastic

cap on the type shown in **FIG 4:93** to renew the bulb.

On De-luxe models, reach the warning light bulbs by removing the facia panel as shown in **FIG 7:63**. **Disconnect the battery first.** Pull the speedo-meter forward to locate the bulb holders. On Super-De-luxe models the bulb holders are a push-fit in sockets behind the instrument panel. On those models where access is obviously not going to be so simple, the work must be entrusted to a dealer.

If there is no fault with the warning bulbs but they still do not work when the indicator switch is operated, check the flasher circuit wiring, the fuse and then the flasher unit as follows:

Checking flasher unit:

On early models the unit is mounted in the engine compartment (see **FIG 7:6**). On Mk 2 models it is behind the facia, being accessible from the parcel tray (see **FIG 7:64**). It is not secured in any way but is simply retained by the two wires. The location is to the right of the facia centre. Take care not to disturb the rest of the wiring that surrounds the unit.

Take extra care when fitting a new unit or it may be damaged by a shortcircuit. Check the wiring first by switching on the ignition. Remove all the leads from the old unit and connect them together. Operate the indicator switch both ways. There is a fault in the wiring if the fuse blows. If all is well, fit the new unit, taking care to connect the wires correctly. Note that the latest type of unit has only two terminal tags instead of the original three (see **FIG 7:64**).

Wiper motor does not run:

First check the fuse between fuse box terminals 3 and 4. If the fuse is sound, switch on the ignition and the wiper and connect the test lamp between fuse box terminal 3 and a clean earth on the body. If the lamp does not light up there is a wiring fault. If the lamp lights on both terminals 3 and 4 there is a fault in the wiper motor, the wiper switch or the wiring between them.

Horn inoperative:

Check the fuse between fuse box terminals 1 and 2. If satisfactory, check the wires and connections to the horn. Also check the horn fixing bolts. The horn must not touch any adjacent part of the car. If the interior light works, there is nothing wrong with the fuse.

To adjust the horn to see whether the fault lies there, short across fuse 1 to 2 with a piece of wire (see **FIG 7:65**). **When pressing the horn switch, do it only momentarily.** If two horns are fitted, remove and insulate the leads to the one not being adjusted. **These leads must not touch surrounding metalwork.** Turn the small serrated screw forward and back for a quarter of a turn to find out if the horn will sound (see **FIG 7:66**). If it does, turn the screw until the horn just fails to sound, then turn back the screw for a quarter of a turn. If the horn will not sound, there is a fault in the horn, the horn push or the wiring. Remember to remove the wire across the 1 to 2 fuse. **When adjusting a horn do not turn the central screw or its locknut.**

Other equipment inoperative:

Failure of the gauges, the heater motor, the rear screen heater, or the tachometer (revolution indicator) may be due to a blown fuse across terminals 3

and 4. Equipment that works independently of the ignition switch will be connected to fuse box terminal 2, so check the 1 to 2 fuse in case of failure. Car radios have a separate fuse, probably in one of the wiring cables. If the fuses are sound, the equipment and wiring needs expert attention.

7:16 Punctures

If a tyre loses air, either in a sudden blow-out or more slowly, the puncture will usually have to be repaired by a tyre specialist or a service station. Sometimes, however, air is lost through a leaking valve. Check for this as shown in **FIG 7:67**. To change a valve core use the special tool sold with the spares. Engage the slots with the valve and unscrew. **Do not screw in a new valve too tightly.**

7:17 Faults in bodywork
Paintwork:

Small dents and scratches may be touched-up using spray-cans of paint. There is always the risk that the new paint make look a different colour because paintwork changes colour with age.

If the dent needs filling, remove all silicone polish from the surrounding surface, using a proprietary solution. Equally effective is a gentle rubbing with 400 grade 'Wet-or-Dry' paper. This is waterproof emerypaper that is sold by accessory shops and is best used with plenty of water.

Buy some paste filler and apply to the dent. A piece of celluloid may be used to level off the filler. Being flexible, the celluloid is readily adjusted to the curvature of body panels. Use the 'Wet-or-Dry' paper and plenty of water to level off the filler. Apply a spray of undercoating after drying off. Rub this down and apply a second coat. Rub down again. When satisfied that the surface is quite smooth apply the finishing coat. Keep it wet in the centre and dry round the edges. Rub it down when dry and do this for two or three coats. Do not spray thickly as it causes runs. Let the paint get thoroughly dry, then use a cutting compound to remove the dry spray round the edges. A compound is sold specially for this purpose. Finally, bring the paint to a high gloss with metal polish.

Windscreen leaks:

Accessory shops sell sealer for curing leaks. Lift the rubber lip round the screen with a wooden wedge and clear out all dirt. **Make sure the recess is dry.** Apply the sealer and wipe the surplus off the glass.

indscreen scratches:

Fine scratches made by the wiper blades can
eliminated by using one of the compounds
vertised in the motoring press.

oor rattles:

Check the security of the hinge screws (see **FIG
:68**). If rattling persists try moving the striker plate
wards (see **Section 4:23, Chapter 4**). Scribe
und the plate before moving it, so that it may be
stored to its original position if there is no improve-
ent.

ccess to door mechanism:

It is useful to be able to remove the trim pad from
e door if the winder or lock mechanism needs
brication. Spraying the inside of the door panel
ith rust-proofing compound is also possible.

Remove the interior handles (see **FIG 7:68**).
emove the door pull and the armrest on Princess
ars. Remove the map pocket (screws in the top
orners). On Princess cars remove any screws
olding the trim pad to the door. On all models insert
screwdriver under the edge of the pad and prise it
way. Plastic tubing over the screwdriver shank will
revent damage to the paintwork (see **FIG 7:69**).

The pad is easily refitted by aligning the spring
lips with the holes in the door and banging them
ome with a light blow of the fist (see inset in **FIG
:69**). Fit the door lock handle at the correct angle.

Bonnet rattles:

These may be due to free play at the front catch.
he central bolt is adjustable. Unlock the nut shown
n **FIG 7:70** and screw the bolt upwards by means
f the slot in the head. Lock the nut and check.

ubrication:

Apply oil to the top of the hinges and work the
loor to and fro as the oil runs down. Grease the
ontact parts of door striker plates and bonnet and
oot lid catches. Keep oil off rubber surrounds. Wipe
ff surplus oil or grease if it is likely to soil clothing.

7:18 Push or tow starting

When automatic transmission is fitted:

Cars fitted with the latest automatic transmission
cannot be tow-started. Cars with engines bearing the
following type numbers may be push- or tow-started.
The numbers are 12H.111, 12H.112, 12H.115 and
12H.116.

The method is to select N, switch on the ignition,
set the mixture control (if necessary), and release
the handbrake. When the road speed is about
20 mile/hr, select second and press the accelerator
pedal enough to start.

When manual transmission is fitted:

A battery that is almost fully-discharged may
not operate the starter motor but may be able to
power the ignition system if the car is push- or tow-
started. In each case, engage top gear with the
clutch out, switch on the ignition, set the mixture
control (if necessary), and in the case of a tow-start,
arrange to sound the horn as an indication that the
towing vehicle should stop. Take care not to run into
the back of the tow. When the car has reached a good
speed (according to the assistance available), let the
clutch in quickly and be ready to push it out again
and to apply the brakes when the engine fires. Try to
push-start downhill, if it is possible.

7:19 Doing even more by yourself

Having come this far, you may well feel that it is
worth doing more involved servicing and repairs on
your car. The money which may be saved and the
satisfaction of knowing that the work has been
thoroughly and properly done has led a third of
to-day's motorists to become do-it-yourself en-
thusiasts. Many of these rely on an Autobook for
detailed, accurate instructions.

Autobooks may be obtained from:

AUTOBOOKS LTD., Golden Lane, Brighton BN1
2QJ, or by ringing Brighton (0273) 721721 for
immediate despatch. The price is £2.50, postage
and packing free, by cheque or P.O. (cheques to be
crossed and made payable to Autobooks Ltd.).
Every Autobook is covered by a guarantee of complete satisfaction or a refund of the full price.

FACTS AND FIGURES

8:1 Engine data   8:2 Fuel system   8:3 Ignition system   8:4 Clutch
8:5 Transmission   8:6 Steering   8:7 Suspension   8:8 Brakes   8:9 Wheels and tyres
8:10 Electrical system   8:11 Capacities   8:12 Dimensions and weights   8:13 Lubrication
Chart

8:1 Engine data

1100—manual gearchange:

Type	10H, 10AMW, 10GR or 10V
Cubic capacity	1098 cubic centimetres (cc)
Compression ratio	8.5:1 (8.9:1, twin carburetters)

1100—automatic transmission:

Type	10AG, 10H
Cubic capacity	1098 cubic centimetres (cc)
Compression ratio	8.9:1

1300:

Type	12G or 12H
Cubic capacity	1275 cubic centimetres (cc)
Compression ratio:	
Austin, Morris (other models to 1968)	8.8:1
MG and Riley after 1968	9.75:1

All models:

Number of cylinders	4
Location of No. 1 cylinder	Nearest to fan
Firing order	1, 3, 4, 2
Valve rocker clearance (cold)	Twelve thousandths of an inch (.012)
Idling speed:	
Manual gearchange	550 revolutions per minute approx.
Automatic transmission	650 revolutions per minute approx.
Oil pressure:	
Normal running	60 pounds per square inch
Idling (minimum)	15 pounds per square inch

8:2 Fuel system

Carburetter type:

1100, manual gearchange	SU, HS2 (single or twin)
1100 and 1300, automatic transmission	SU, HS4 (single)
1300 manual gearchange	SU, HS4 (single) or HS2 (twin)

Piston needle marking:

1100 manual gearchange:

Standard	AN (single), D3 (twin)
Weak	EB (single), GV (twin)
Rich	H6 (single), D6 (twin)

1100 and 1300 automatic transmission:

Standard	DL
Weak	ED
Rich	BQ

1300, single carburetter:

Standard	DZ
Weak	CF
Rich	BQ

1300, twin carburetters:

Standard	EB (low compression ratio)
	GY (high compression ratio)
Weak	GG
Rich	M

Piston spring colour:

Single carburetter	Red
Twin carburetters	Blue

Fuel pump:

Type	SU, electric
Model	SP (early 1100), AUF 200 or AUF 204 (later)

8:3 Ignition system

Sparking plugs:

Type:

1100	Champion N5
1300	Champion N9Y
Gap (all models)	24 to 26 thousandths of an inch (.024 to .026)

Ignition coil type:

All models except 1300 with high compression ratio	LA12
1300 with high compression ratio of 9.75:1	HA12

Distributor:

Type	25D4
Rotation	Anticlockwise, viewed from above
Contact breaker gap	14 to 16 thousandths of an inch (.014 to .016)

Static ignition timing:

1100, manual gearchange:
Single carburetter engine ... ... 3 deg. BTDC
Twin carburetter engine ... ... 5 deg. BTDC
1100 and 1300, automatic transmission:
With distributor No. 41134A ... ... 7 deg. BTDC
With distributor No. 41181A ... ... 5 deg. BTDC
1300, single or twin carburetter and 8.8:1 compression ratio:
With distributor No. 41214 or 41257 ... ... 8 deg. BTDC (single)
With distributor No. 41134, 41251 or 41242 ... ... 5 deg. BTDC (twin)
1300, twin carburetter and 9.75:1 compression ratio:
With distributor No. 41238 ... ... 3 deg. BTDC
Note: BTDC means Before top dead centre

Stroboscopic ignition timing:

With engine at 600 rev/min and vacuum pipe disconnected:
1100, manual gearchange:
Single carburetter engine ... ... 5 deg. BTDC
Twin carburetter engine ... ... 7 deg. BTDC
1100 and 1300, automatic transmission:
With distributor No. 41134A ... ... 10 deg. BTDC
With distributor No. 41181A ... ... 8 deg. BTDC
1300, single or twin carburetters and 8.8:1 compression ratio:
With distributor No. 41214 or 41257 ... ... 10 deg. BTDC (single)
With distributor No. 41134, 41251 or 41242 ... ... 8 deg. BTDC (twin)
1300, twin carburetters and 9.75:1 compression ratio:
With distributor No. 41238 ... ... 5 deg. BTDC

Timing marks:

Location ... ... On flywheel. Fixed pointer on clutch housing

8:4 Clutch
Hydraulic fluid ... ... Lockheed Disc Brake Fluid, Series 2 or 329

8:5 Transmission
Manual gearbox:
Number of speeds... ... ... 4 forward, one reverse
Synchromesh ... ... Second, third and top (early 1100). All forward gears (later 1100 and all 1300)

8:6 Steering

Tracking of front wheels ... ... $\frac{1}{16}$ inch toe-out

8:7 Suspension
Trim height ... ... $13\frac{5}{8}$ inch, plus or minus $\frac{1}{4}$ inch (measured from centre of hub cap to top of wheel arch)

8:8 Brakes

Type:

Front	...	...	...	...	...	...	Disc
Rear	...	...	...	...	...	...	Drum
Footbrake ...	...	...	...	...	...	...	Hydraulic, all four wheels
Handbrake	...	...	...	...	...	...	Cable operated mechanical on rear wheels only
Brake fluid	...	...	...	...	...	...	Lockheed Disc Brake Fluid, Series 2 or 329

8:9 Wheels and tyres

Wheels	...	...	...	...	...	...	4J x 12 (Mk 1), 4C x 12 (Mk 2 and 1300)

Tyres:

Size	...	...	...	...	...	...	5.50 x 12 (cross-ply) 145SR x 12 (radial-ply)

Pressure in pounds per square inch (cold):

Front (all models)	...	...	...	...	...	28 (cross-ply), 32 (radial-ply)
Rear (saloon)	...	...	...	...	...	24 (cross-ply), 28 (radial-ply)
Rear (Countryman and Traveller)	...	...	...	...	26 (cross-ply), 28 (radial-ply)

8:10 Electrical system

Battery:

Type:

Early models	...	...	...	...	...	...	12-volt Lucas N9 or NZ9
Later models	...	...	...	...	...	...	12-volt Lucas D9 or DZ9
Earthing system	...	...	...	...	...	...	Positive (+) terminal connected to body (but negative (−) if later alternator 16ACR is fitted)

Starter motor:

Type ...	...	...	...	...	...	...	Lucas M35G or M35J

Generator (dynamo):

Type ...	...	...	...	...	...	...	Lucas C40

Alternator (alternative to generator):

Type:

Positive earth	...	...	...	...	...	...	Lucas 11AC
Negative earth	...	...	...	...	...	...	Lucas 16ACR

Note: Ensure correct type and polarity when servicing or when fitting a radio

Lamp bulbs (12-volt):

	Watts	BLMC part number
Headlamps (sealed beam, righthand drive)	50/40	BFS.414
Sidelamps (not Princess)	6	GLB.989
Sidelamps, Princess	5	GLB.501
Direction Indicators (front and rear)	21	GLB.382
Tail and stop lights	6/21	GLB.380
Number plate lamp, Morris and MG	6	BFS.207
Number plate lamp, Austin, Wolseley, Princess and Riley ...	6	GLB.989
Panel and warning lights (screw-in)	2.2	GLB.987
Panel and warning lights (bayonet)	2	GLB.281
Interior light	6	GLB.254
Direction indicator arm	1.5	BFS.280
Radiator badge (Wolseley)	6	GLB.989
Fog lamp (Princess)	48	BFS.323
Reversing lamp (Princess)	21	GLB.382
Wing valance repeater lamps:		
Capless	5	GLB.501
Bayonet fixing	6	GLB.989
Direction indicator warning lights (later)	2.2	GLB.987
Number plate lamp, later Austin, Morris, Princess, Riley 1300, Wolseley 1300, MG, Riley 1300 Mk 2, Wolseley 1300 Mk 2 ...	6	GLB.207

8:11 Capacities

Transmission casing (manual gearchange)	$8\frac{1}{2}$ pints including filter
Filter	1 pint
Automatic transmission casing and filter	13 pints (refill 9 pints)
Cooling system without heater	$5\frac{3}{4}$ pints
Heater	1 pint
Fuel tank	8 gallons

8:12 Dimensions and weights:

Length	12 ft $2\frac{3}{4}$ inches
Width	5 ft $0\frac{3}{8}$ inches
Height	4 ft 5 inches
Weight in kerbside trim:	
Saloon (manual gearchange)	1782 lb
Saloon (automatic transmission)	1848 lb
Countryman and Traveller	1820 lb

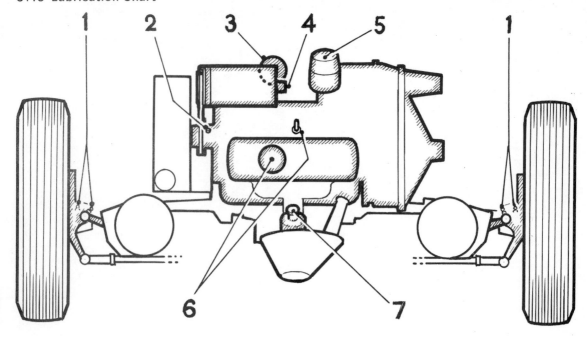

Lubrication chart showing location of principal parts needing periodic attention. The specific intervals or milages for such attention are given below.

Weekly:

Check engine oil level at dipstick. Replenish, if necessary, at filler cap 6 using fresh 20W/50 oil.

Every 3000 miles (5000 km) or 3 months:

Give 3 or 4 strokes of grease gun to steering joint nipples 1, using Multi-purpose grease. Use engine oil to top-up the carburetter damper chamber at 7 to the correct level if required. On engines with automatic transmission, drain the old oil and refill with fresh engine oil and fit a new oil filter element 3.

Every 6000 miles (10,000 km) or 6 months:

On engines with manual gearchange, drain the old oil. Refill with fresh 20W/50 oil at filler cap 6. Lubricate distributor 5 (see Chapter 5). Add few drops of engine oil to end bearing of generator at 4 (do not over-oil). Fit new oil filter element 3.

Every 12,000 miles (20,000 km) or 12 months:

Remove plug 2 from water pump body (early models only). Insert a very small quantity of multi-purpose grease and refit screw.

Note:

If lubrication warning light glows, fit a new oil filter element 3 and change the engine/transmission oil. When automatic transmission is fitted do not put additives in the lubricating oil.

NOTES

9

THE MEANING OF—

This glossary explains certain technical terms that may prove baffling to the uninitiated.

Advancing and retarding ignition Altering the ignition firing point so that it occurs earlier or later in the engine cycle of operation

AF 'American Fine', a system of nut, bolt and thread sizes. The width across the flats of bolt head or nut is used to identify the appropriate spanner

Air filter A car engine uses large volumes of air, some of it dirty. An air filter traps this dirt to prevent it causing excessive engine wear

Alternator A belt-driven generator of electricity. Smaller than the earlier form of generator, it is also simpler and gives a higher output at low speeds

Autobook The amateur's guide to maintenance, servicing and repairs on a particular car. Written and illustrated in easy-to-follow, step-by-step instructions. Covers the overhaul of every component and includes fault diagnosis tables. Suitable for the DIY motorist with only elementary mechanical knowledge (see **Section 7:19**)

Bendix pinion Self-engaging pinion on starter motor shaft. Engages with flywheel gear

Brushes Spring-loaded carbon blocks used in generators and starter motors to transfer electricity to or from a rotating part

Capacitor Modern term for electrical condenser. Absorbs electrical charges and prevents excessive sparking across contact breaker points in distributor

Carburetter A device for providing a mixture of petrol and air in correct proportions. This is fired in the engine to produce power.

Centrifugal advance Mechanism consisting of spring loaded weights in the distributor that advances the moment of ignition as the engine speed increases

Choke Manual or automatic control of carburetter to provide a rich mixture for starting from cold

Coil A component in the ignition or firing system that steps-up the 12-volt supply from the battery to the high voltage needed to produce sparks at the sparking plug points

Compression ratio A measure of the pressure put on the petrol/air mixture in the engine. High-compression engines give greater performance but need better petrols

Condenser Earlier name for capacitor, as used in the distributor

Contact breaker An electrical switch in the ignition distributor that makes and breaks the 12-volt supply from the battery to the coil

Cylinder head The top part of the engine that houses the valves, the sparking plugs and also carries the inlet and exhaust pipe manifolds

Damper Modern term for shock-absorber, used in vehicle suspension systems to damp out spring oscillations

Decarbonizing Also known as a 'decoke'. The removal of carbon deposits that build up inside an engine after long periods of use. These deposits reduce the performance of the engine

Disc brakes   A flat-disc revolves with the road wheel. Friction pads are pressed against both faces of the disc when the brake pedal is depressed

Distributor   Is driven by the engine to operate the contact breaker and then distribute the resulting current from the coil to each sparking plug in the correct firing order

Drum brakes   An open-sided drum revolves with the road wheel. Inside it, stationary friction-lined shoes may be expanded into braking contact with the inner curved surface

Dynamo   The earlier name for a generator of electricity. Is driven by belt from the engine

Earthing   The electrical supply from the battery must make a complete circuit through the equipment to be operated, and then back to the battery. One wire is used to start off the circuit and the return to the battery is made by earthing through the steel framework of the car

Electrodes   Metal points with a small gap between, across which a spark can jump, as in sparking plugs

Electrolyte   A dilute solution of sulphuric acid in distilled water. Used in car batteries

EP   Extreme pressure. In lubricants, special grades for heavily loaded surfaces such as gear teeth in a gearbox or the crownwheel and pinion in a rear axle

Fade   Of brakes. Reduced efficiency due to overheating

Firing order   As the engine operates, each one of its four cylinders will compress a petrol/air mixture in turn. This mixture is fired by a sparking plug. The four plugs are arranged to fire in a particular order so that a smooth flow of power is obtained

Fuse   The weak link in an electrical circuit. A wire in the fuse melts when excessive current passes through it, thus breaking the electrical circuit

Gasket   A thin sheet of slightly-compressible material used to prevent leakage between metal surfaces

Generator   Modern term for dynamo. Device driven by belt from the engine to produce electricity for battery charging and for the electrical equipment

Grommet   A ring of protective or sealing material used to protect pipes or leads passing through a panel

Halfshaft   One of a pair of shafts transmitting drive from the differential to the rear wheels

High compression   See 'Compression ratio'

High-tension   A reference to the high electrical voltages that are needed to produce sparks at the sparking plugs. High-tension systems are heavily insulated to avoid the risk of leakage and shock

Hydraulic operation   The use of a liquid in a pipe to transmit pressure. Used in brake and clutch systems

Hydrolastic   Name for suspension system used on 1100 and 1300 models. Rubber springs are combined with a fluid-filled system linking front and rear suspension

Hydrometer   A device for checking the specific gravity of liquids. Used to check the condition of battery electrolyte

Inlet manifold   Branched pipework that conducts the petrol/air mixture from the carburetter to the engine

Loom   A fabric casing that makes a neat enclosure of several electrical wires

Low compression   See 'Compression ratio'

Low-tension   The current output from the battery

Manifold   A pipe, duct or chamber, with several branches

Master cylinder   A device for transmitting pedal pressure to a fluid that moves along a system of pipes to brake and clutch mechanisms

Octane number   Numbered scale used to indicate the grade of petrol. High octane fuels cost more and are necessary for high performance engines with a high compression ratio

Oil bath   In air filters, a reservoir of oil for wetting a wire mesh element to hold the dust

Oil filter   A fine strainer that removes foreign particles from the engine lubricating oil

Oil wetted   In air filters, a wire mesh element lightly oiled during servicing to trap airborne dust

Pinion   A small gear, usually in mesh with another, larger gear

Pinking   A light tinkling sound from an engine that is pulling hard under load when running on inferior petrol or with an ignition (firing) point that is too far advanced. It may also happen if the engine needs decarbonizing

Ring gear   A gear tooth ring attached to the outer periphery of the flywheel. Starter pinion engages with it during starting

Running-on   The phenomenon is that of an engine that continues to fire after the ignition is switched off. Frequently due to glowing deposits of carbon in the cylinder head

Shock absorber See 'Damper'

Solenoid A coil actuated by a small electric current to operate contacts or a mechanical device. Used to switch on the heavy current to the starter motor

Squab The backrest of a seat

Synchromesh Mechanism in the gearbox that facilitates gear changing by matching the speeds of the engaging gears

Tachometer Instrument that shows the speed of an engine in revolutions per minute

TDC Stands for 'Top Dead Centre' which is a particular point in the cycle of engine operations. May be preceded by B or A standing for 'Before' or 'After'

Thermostat A temperature-operated device that opens or closes a valve to control the passage of engine cooling water. Used to give a rapid warm-up from cold

Toe-out The front wheels are not parallel, but toe-out when viewed from above. That is, the distance between the wheels is greater at the front that at the back, measured at wheel centre height

Universal joint Joints inserted in the drive shafts to the front wheels. These continue to transmit the drive from the gearbox even at the angles produced by steering or suspension movements

Vacuum advance and retard Mechanism in the distributor that is operated by pressure changes in the inlet manifold. This movement is used to advance or retard the moment of ignition or firing (see 'Advancing and retarding ignition' and 'Inlet manifold')

Vacuum Servo Device sometimes fitted in the brake system, using the difference between atmospheric pressure and inlet manifold depression to operate a piston which acts to increase brake pressure as required

Water pump A fan-like impeller, driven by belt from the engine, that keeps water circulating in the cooling system

Watt A unit of electrical power. Used to identify the output of lamp bulbs

Wheel cylinder Cylinder with hydraulically operated piston or pistons acting on brake shoes or pads